SO
YOU
WANT
TO BE
A
SPORTSCASTER

SO YOU WANT TO BE A Sportscaster

THE TECHNIQUES AND SKILLS
OF SPORTS ANNOUNCING
BY ONE OF THE COUNTRY'S
MOST EXPERIENCED BROADCASTERS

Ken Coleman

An Associated Features Book

HAWTHORN BOOKS, INC.
PUBLISHERS / *New York*

To Ellen

Contents

	Preface	ix
	Acknowledgment	xi
	Introduction by Sidney B. McKeen	xiii
1	*How It All Began*	3
2	*Baseball*	14
3	*Football*	32
4	*Basketball*	49
5	*Hockey*	57
6	*Golf*	65
7	*A Sporting Variety*	72
8	*The Daily and Weekly Sports Show*	80
9	*The Art of Interviewing*	93
10	*The Announcer Wears Many Hats*	103
11	*The Role of the Former Athlete*	112
12	*Producing and Directing*	117
13	*Well-known Announcers and How They Got That Way*	123
14	*Bouquets and Brickbats*	135
15	*Playback*	143
16	*How Do You Get Started?*	150
	Index	159

Preface

A soldier in Vietnam wrote me that he had been a claims adjuster before entering the army but that when he was discharged, he wanted to become a sportscaster. How did he go about it?

A high-school junior wrote, "During this past year I have looked into colleges that offer courses in broadcasting. Because of your extensive background in this field I felt that you would be able to give me the necessary information."

A thirty-five-year-old Ivy League college graduate, an executive with a small manufacturing company, wanted to know, "Should I try to obtain some formal training first, or is it possible to break in immediately and receive on-the-job training to become a radio and television sportscaster?"

An Army man stationed in the Canal Zone wrote, "I have done a year of football and basketball play-by-play and was the sports director for a small station in Minnesota. However, I feel I lack that professional touch. Could you suggest some books to read or any other information that might help me put a better show on the air?"

A student from Bentley College in Waltham, Massachusetts, wanted to know the effect broadcasting has on a man's family life: "Is sports announcing a well-paying field, and can a basic salary meet the cost of living?"

I guess hardly a day goes by that I don't receive letters like these from aspiring broadcasters. I answer them all.

But one thing I discovered along the way was that I couldn't find any books on sportscasting to recommend. There are how-to books on just about every subject under the sun, but to the best of my knowledge there has never been a book on sportscasting by a working professional. If the telephone calls and letters of inquiry that I receive are typical of the sort that broadcasters receive throughout the country—and I found they are—then this is demonstration enough that a book on the subject is essential.

And that is how I came to write it.

K. C.
Cohasset, Massachusetts

Acknowledgment

I'd like to thank Ray Fitzgerald, sports columnist of the Boston *Globe,* for his encouragement and invaluable aid in the preparation of this manuscript.

K. C.

Introduction

Photo by Bradford F. Andersen

Meet Ken Coleman, as seen in this play-by-play account written by Sidney B. McKeen in the summer of 1970 for the Worcester, Massachusetts, Sunday Telegram.

The mod-looking young man in the headset leans over Ken Coleman's shoulder and presses a crinkled, dog-eared index card into his palm. The card is entitled "Red Sox Disclaimer." It's easy to see it's been around.

Coleman speaks the words, half reading from the card, but his eyes are straying out across the expanse of green that is Fenway Park. "This program," he says, "is authorized under telecasting rights granted by the Boston Red Sox solely for the entertainment of our audience, and any publication, rebroadcast, or other use of the pictures, descriptions, and accounts of this game without the express written consent of the Boston Red Sox is prohibited."

That litany, hard on the heels of the national anthem, Coleman could recite in his sleep. The "pictures, descriptions, and accounts" of Red Sox baseball games are his meat and potatoes, his on- and off-field obsession from April through September every year.

"Gee, those guys have the cushiest job in the world," fans have been heard to remark with a jerk of the thumb in the direction of the radio and television booth up on the roof behind home plate. But a day up there with Coleman and his two partners—Ned Martin and Johnny Pesky—is likely to convince you otherwise. It did for me one Sunday afternoon in June when the Sox and the Kansas City Royals squared off in a doubleheader.

The day begins early. At 8:30, a full five hours before the opener, the Channel 5 camera crews, engineers, and production assistants have already started electronic preparations. An engineer from Kansas City is unpacking just overhead to get ready for a radio account back to the visitors' home city.

There's good-natured banter over hot coffee among the men who work the four cameras—located in the TV booth, upstairs behind third base, at the corner of the Sox dugout, and in faraway center field. They go over game plans in much the same way as the ballplayers. Camera 2 in the booth will follow the ball for the entire game. Camera 1 on the third-base side will concentrate on close-ups of putouts by outfielders, all the putouts at first base, and at-bat shots of the left-handed hitters. Camera 3 by the dugout will shoot right-handed batters and cover the front runner with more than one on base. Camera 4 in deep center will work on close-ups looking over the pitcher's shoulder and take a glance now and then at their successors-to-be warming up in the bullpen below.

Audio engineer Paul Levin, of Brookline, an old pro with a walrus mustache who started twenty-five years ago with play-by-play announcer Jim Britt, fiddles with some dials.

Coleman arrives at the park from his home in Cohasset a couple of hours before game time. He's doing an on-field description of the annual Fathers and Sons Game over the park's public-address system. Martin, who lives in Wellesley, and Pesky, from Swampscott, arrive by noon and get a quick lunch in the club's dining room on the roof.

All three stop by the clubhouse to check on last-minute details involving the players: Who's hurt and out of the lineup? What about this new kid? What's doing?

By game time Pesky, an ex-Red Sox shortstop and later its manager, has reduced an eight-inch cigar to ashes. Martin, natty in a gold sport coat and coordinated shirt and tie, records a radio commercial for Zayre's that will be played on each broadcast for the next two weeks. Coleman, more tense than the other two, takes up a seat next to Pesky and shuffles through freshly mimeographed statistics about the players on both teams.

At 1:25, Martin is on the air in the radio booth, twenty-five running steps down a narrow passageway from Coleman and Pesky on the TV side. A partition separates them. From here in, only a minute out for commercials at half-inning intervals stands between them and continuous pressurized chatter.

It's 1:30 now, and Martin reads off the starting lineups, checking the names on his own scorecard, which he keeps with a black felt-tip pen. Over on the TV side Coleman has handed his index card with its solemn "disclaimer" back to the production assistant on the stool behind him.

The production man scratches out the first line of a long list of scheduled commercials. Schaefer Beer has the first three innings, the Boston *Herald Traveler* the middle three, and National Shawmut Bank the last three. Most of it is film projected at the studios on Morrissey Boulevard, in Dorchester.

The beer commercial over, the production assistant waves his hand and Coleman launches into his play-by-play. The Royals get two hits off Gary Peters but no runs.

1:44 P.M. Dave Morehead, formerly with Boston, warms up for Kansas City.

Coleman: "Johnny, you're the man who gave Dave his first start in the major leagues, isn't that right?"

Pesky: "That's right, Ken; he was just a youngster then, right out of high school. He pitched some fine baseball for us, too. He's always had a great arm."

Coleman (looking at a mimeographed fact sheet): "Morehead, on the twenty-fifth day of May, pitched his best ball game of the year, going all the way against the White Sox and giving up just three scratch singles."

Pesky: "He's in great physical shape this year . . . matter of fact, the thinnest I can remember seeing him."

Sitting at Coleman's left is his cousin, Charley Linnett. Charley, from Canton, is a Red Sox fan, a self-employed commercial artist and a whiz with facts and figures. On all Red Sox home stands, Coleman pays him out of his own pocket to feed him statistical data. Linnett, stout and scholarly-looking, is armed with books and a personal memory bank that bulges at the seams.

1:50. Mike Andrews and Reggie Smith reach base safely, and with nobody out, Carl Yastrzemski strides menacingly to the plate. Linnett, reading from the *Official Baseball*

Guide, published by the *Sporting News,* scratches out a quick note on a tiny pad of paper and shoves it in front of his cousin:

YAZ

VS KC 69

.283

Coleman: "Carl Yastrzemski stepping in. Carl last year against Kansas City had a batting average of .283."

1:52. Yaz swings hard and sends a foul ball back at the booth, and it hits like a rocket and "wooooops" back down the screen to the field of action. Linnett pens another note to Coleman, giving the date of a no-hitter Morehead once pitched for the Red Sox at Fenway Park. Ken skillfully weaves it into his patter as Yastrzemski takes ball four.

1:54. Tony Conigliaro lines a single to left, and two runs are home for Boston. Over on the radio side Ned Martin, holding one of the press releases distributed earlier in the dining room, advises his audience that "Tony now moves into the club leadership in RBI's."

While Kansas City warms up a new pitcher, William Koster, executive director of the Jimmy Fund, a children's cancer-research drive, shows up and hands Coleman a note: "We have the foremen and supervisors of Sealol, Inc., of Warwick, Rhode Island, here as a group each year, and they always bring a fine contribution for the Jimmy Fund."

Over on the radio side, engineer Al Walker, who is constantly kidded on the air about his eating habits, rips ticker tape from a machine at his right elbow and passes it under a screen to Martin. The tape says, "N LA PGH 000 00." Martin quickly converts that into an out-of-town score ("In the National League the Dodgers and Pirates are scoreless at the end of two and a half.")

2:06. Press-box steward Tommy McCarthy, an old-timer around Fenway, comes in as Tom Satriano grounds out to end the inning, and McCarthy hands out hot chocolate and iced Coke. It's a cold, cloudy day, and the hot chocolate goes first. Coleman doesn't have time to finish his. The production man in the headset, holding a stopwatch on the commercial from the studios, waves a hand, says, "Ten seconds, Ken," and takes away the drink.

2:30. A night light flashes, and a buzzer goes off. It's Walker cuing Martin to a station break.

2:36. A forced play ends the Kansas City third after Pat Kelly's home run into the Red Sox bullpen, and while the Sox are batting, with a lull on the field, Walker hands Martin a page of mimeographed "drop-ups"—commercials to be used within innings ("Know what the quality is that sets Schaefer apart from other beers? Consistency . . .").

2:45. The Sox go down in the third, and Martin and Coleman quickly exchange booths, Ken turning from TV to radio, and Ned from radio to TV. Martin doesn't quite make it to the TV side in time, and Pesky calls one strike on Jim Campanis, leading off the Royals' fourth. "All right, John," says Martin, winded and taking over. "What do you think, a nine o'clock dinner tonight?"

Kansas City goes down quickly, and during the studio commercial Martin and Pesky kid around for fifty seconds. "Brewster-the-Rooster, you look beautiful today," shouts Pesky, admiring Martin's sport coat.

3:12. Over on the radio side Coleman gets into a coughing spell. Al Walker cuts his mike until it clears up. Ken explains later that the pregame festivities on the PA strained his voice. "Happens about once a month," he says.

3:24. The Royals' Jackie Hernandez ties the game with a home run into the left-field screen, and Lee Stange is summoned from the Red Sox bullpen. On the TV side Pesky has an envelope full of cards telling what each pitcher has done the last time out. The line on Stange reads, "31-

Chi-2⅔-5-4-1-1-1-2 'not so good,' " meaning that on May 31 he pitched two and two thirds innings against Chicago, giving up five hits and four runs, walking one, and striking out one, and that he's won one game, lost two, and that last outing was not one of his better ones.

3:30. Bob Oliver comes to bat, swinging a dark-brown, almost black bat. Charley Linnett scribbles a quick note to Martin: "That dark bat rare?" Martin then notes the color of the bat to the TV audience, and Johnny Pesky tells about the time Goose Goslin, the old Tiger outfielder, tried to use a striped bat and the umpires wouldn't let him. Johnny chuckles about it.

3:33. The sun makes a brief appearance, and Tommy McCarthy does, too, with a second round of hot chocolate and soft drinks. Pesky pulls a package of Saran Wrap from his coat. Salami. He hands the slices around. Audio man Levin tries it and fans his mouth. It's hot, and there are few takers.

3:40. Linnett hands Martin a note: "Stange pitched to 5 men in one full inning, 0 hits, 0 runs." Martin doesn't use it. "I don't like too many statistics," he confides later.

3:53. The Red Sox go out in the sixth after getting two go-ahead runs. Martin decides he wants Tony Conigliaro, who has three hits now, as his guest on the postgame show, *Red Sox Wrap-up with Ned Martin.* The production man sends word down to the dugout to have Tony hang on.

4:19. Red Sox relief pitcher Ken Brett is at bat, only his second trip all year. "I remember a game against the Yankees when Ken had a single, double, and triple," Martin, back on the radio side, tells the fans. On the next pitch Brett clubs a home run into the Sox bullpen.

Consulting nothing but his memory, Martin calls it the third home run this year by a Red Sox pitcher. A minute later he finds what he's looking for in an old ledger book filled with his own notes and announces that Jim Lonborg and Vicente Romo hit the other two, citing dates and opponents.

4:27. The eighth is over. Pesky, off the air, yahoos in exultation over Brett's home run: "Did he ever tattoo that one . . . boy, did he ever!"

Martin says he doesn't see his function as a cheerleader on the air. "If somebody messes it up, I don't see why I shouldn't say so. It's different in some towns like Chicago, where they do a certain amount of that, but New England fans wouldn't stand for it."

4:34. The game is over. The Red Sox win it, 7 to 4. Pesky hustles from the TV side to take the mike and give the summary so Martin can race down to the field for his postgame interview with Conigliaro.

4:40. Pesky and Coleman make themselves sandwiches in the rooftop dining room, occasionally glancing up at the color TV set, which shows Martin talking to Tony down on the field.

4:55. Coleman, Martin, and Pesky crowd into the radio booth to start the play-by-play of the second game—TV is not covering this one.

7:35. The second game is over, the Sox winning it 5–2 on an eighth-inning grand-slam homer by Rico Petrocelli.

7:40. Coleman pounds away on a portable typewriter, the beginning of a script for a radio sports show he'll do tomorrow. Why now? "I'm just too tense after a game to head out into the traffic right away. Besides, this has to be done sometime."

Coleman, who grew up in Quincy making up baseball games he broadcast to himself, cupping a hand over his left ear to listen to the sound of his own voice (a habit he never got out of), says he can't imagine doing anything else. "All I want to do is get better at this," he says.

8:15. Coleman, Martin, and Pesky bump into their broadcasting counterpart from Kansas City in the dining room. After a day of talking baseball the four of them talk baseball.

8:30. The Red Sox broadcasting crew heads for the parking lot, where youngsters are fighting mounted policemen for autographs of the players.

Along the Southeast Expressway, a line keeps running through Ken Coleman's head: ". . . and any publication, rebroadcast, or other use of the pictures, descriptions, and accounts of this game without the express written consent of the Boston Red Sox is prohibited."

Tomorrow will be another day.

SO
YOU
WANT
TO BE
A
SPORTSCASTER

CHAPTER 1

How It All Began

The years was 1947, the place was Rutland, Vermont, and the play-by-play announcer on WSYB for the Rutland Royals, of the Northern League, was Ken Coleman. That's where it all began for me. Almost every other sportscaster —excluding the former athletes, of course—can point to some small town on the map and say the same thing.

I had actually gone on the air a year earlier, on a program called *Veterans Job Center of the Air,* over WEEI in Boston. I was attending Curry College, a school for prospective broadcasters, and was picked to announce job opportunities for veterans. I remember walking on Tremont Street after the show and thinking that everybody was looking at me because I had just done something important. I had this feeling even though there wasn't a soul on the street.

In Rutland the WSYB studios were over a paint store. There were four staff announcers who, as they say about athletes today, could do it all. Or at least, they were assigned to do it all—from soap commercials to newscasts to time checks to record shows to sports assignments.

Let me recount my first game, a chain of misfortune from the time I arrived at the field.

It was the Royals against the Bennington Generals at

3

Ken Coleman gets the word from Carl Yastrzemski.

St. Peter's Field. Game time was 1:30 and I was there in plenty of time, arriving at 10 A.M. Nobody else showed up for an hour and a half.

The engineer, as a matter of fact, didn't arrive until there were two outs in the top of the first. It is very difficult—in fact, impossible—to do a broadcast without an engineer, so my sports debut included doing a half-inning recap.

It began to rain in the second inning. In the majors today when it rains, you chit-chat with your color man or call in a guest or two for a discussion of the finer points of the game.

But at St. Peter's Field that spring day in 1947, I was alone. I "filled" for forty-five minutes, talking to myself on a variety of subjects. Someone once said Mel Allen could fill fifteen minutes during a rain delay debating the pros and cons of the infield fly rule. Mel had nothing on me that day.

The rain stopped, play resumed, and I moved along until the fourth, when it began to pour again. I gave the folks of Rutland some more of my expertise and then the game was called. My first ball game had gone down the drain.

I probably made a thousand mistakes that day, but at least I had something going for me. I had grown up listening to all kinds of sports broadcasters. There had been men before me to set a pattern.

The pioneers in the business had no such pattern. They couldn't go back in their minds and think: "Let's see, this is the way it was done in the 1917 World Series." They were on their own, with no guidelines, armed only with their own ingenuity and wit.

Consider, for example, the announcer for WJZ who would break an ordinary kitchen match close to the mike in such a way that it sounded like a bat smacking a baseball. The same man, wearing a set of earphones, would get a description of the game over the telephone from the park. He would then describe the play over his microphone, which was conveniently placed near an open window. Just below the window, on an adjoining rooftop, was a group of hired extras who would cheer and shout upon signal from WJZ.

"The fans are going wild," the announcer would say, hanging his mike out the window to catch the cries of the mercenaries.

Harold Arlin, on KDKA in Pittsburgh, did the first broadcast of a college football game, on November 5, 1921, between Pitt and West Virginia. Arlin yelled so loudly on one touchdown that he knocked the station off the air. It is doubtful that Arlin had spotting boards, statisticians, and an expert alongside.

Grantland Rice, better known for his newspaper work and his verse about not caring whether you won or lost but how you played the game, broadcast the 1921 World Series for KDKA. And someone named J. Andrew White described the Jack Dempsey-Georges Carpentier fight on July 2, 1921, over the air.

The first big name in sports broadcasting was Graham McNamee, whose main job was acting. Then came Ted Husing, Bill Stern, Bill Munday, and Clem McCarthy, and as the business mushroomed, so did the list of nationally known sports announcers.

Red Barber, Mel Allen, Chris Schenkel, Lindsey Nelson, Curt Gowdy, Don Dunphy, Vin Scully, and Ray Scott are just as famous as the men they talk about for a living.

The old radio microphones looked like a round oatmeal box. Often, the announcers broadcast directly from the grandstand, with the paying customers looking on curiously at the freak talking to himself.

Of course, because these men were the first, there was no one to compare them with. Today, you can get into as big an argument over whether Curt Gowdy is better than Ray Scott in broadcasting football as you can over the abilities of the players themselves.

Many of the early broadcasters, frankly, weren't very good. Some were chosen on the basis of their voices, rather than on knowledge of the sport. Some were spellbinding with description but didn't know the basic rules of the game they were talking about.

So how important is it to have a "good" voice? Ideally, a professional sports announcer has a pleasing voice, is a master of the language, and knows his game. However, any sports fan can name broadcasters who have done very well without the booming, mellifluous delivery. Nobody ever did a horse race better than Clem McCarthy, with his rasping commentary. Vin Scully, the darling of the West Coast, has a high voice. Harry Caray and Bob Prince, baseball professionals for years, go so fast they almost break the speed of sound, yet they've made a more than comfortable living.

The important factors in being a broadcaster are knowing the game, reporting it with enthusiasm, and being adaptable to situations that arise.

Television has become the glamor part of the business, but radio is still the medium that uses the audience's imagination. As Detroit *Free Press* sports columnist Joe Falls points out, radio put him in the stands even when he really wasn't there. He could picture the place in his mind and his imagination took it from there.

My generation grew up with radio. People outside New England may never have heard of Fred Hoey, but he was the voice of my youth. Hoey was a pioneer in New England baseball broadcasting.

"Score tied, Mel Almada on second base with two out. There's a single to center and here comes Almada around third. C'mon, Mel, beat the throw. He did it, fans, and the Red Sox win, 4 to 3."

That was Hoey. So was this: "He throws to first and gets his man." Years later I found myself using that same phrase in doing Red Sox baseball.

A friend tells me that instant nostalgia for him is walking past someone's house on a summer's day and hearing the faint sound of a ball game coming from a radio inside. In a flash, he's back to the days of Jimmy Foxx, Doc Cramer, and Eric McNair. And Fred Hoey.

Many young baseball fans have told me they followed the progress of the 1967 pennant race by listening to Ned Martin and me on transistor radios at the beach.

There were other New England broadcasting names in my youth, such as Frank Fallon, who did the Braves games and answered many questions about how to get into the business; Frankie Frisch, the Old Fordham Flash, who also did the Braves one year and whose war cry was "Oh, those bases on balls"; and Jim Britt, whose vocabulary was one of the best in broadcasting.

Frisch, who had a high-pitched voice, interspersed his description of the Braves—a perfectly dreadful team in those days—by giving baseball tips to youngsters. He once pointed out that the way to break in a new glove was to tie a ball in the pocket and stick the mitt in a bucket of water overnight.

Maybe that's the way you broke in a big league glove, but the next morning my $1.95 Lon Warneke model came apart finger by finger as I lifted it from the water.

Britt had a mellow voice, a great knowledge of baseball, and a way with words. In fact, his extensive vocabulary was so good that at times it sounded as though he was talking over the heads of the listeners. I worked with Britt for two years in Cleveland on the Indians' telecasts.

Some of the gimmicks used by the early broadcasters probably wouldn't go over in what we think of as a more sophisticated era. Rosy Rosewall, who preceded Prince as the Pirates' announcer, made a big production out of a Pittsburgh home run. He would have Prince, then his assistant, break a pane of glass and Rosy would shout into the mike: "Watch out, Aunt Minnie, here she comes." The idea was, of course, that the home run had just gone through the window of Aunt Minnie's house out there beyond the fence. Today, this would be super corn, but it worked for Rosewell.

This doesn't mean there aren't gimmicks today. Most of them are verbal, the catch phrase that identifies an announcer. Phil Rizzuto has his "Holy cow," Mel Allen his

"How about that," Harry Caray his "Boy, oh boy," Red Barber his "Oh, Doctor," Bob Elson his *"He's* out."

Before Walter O'Malley acquired Chavez Ravine, the Los Angeles Dodgers played in the Coliseum with a screen in very short left field. When the Pirates came to town, Prince would say at least half a dozen times during the game: "C'mon, Bucs, let's play Screeno."

The danger in these verbal trademarks is that they grow stale through overuse. You have to be sure that repetition won't grate on the very listeners you're trying to entertain.

Today's sports fan seldom if ever hears the re-created broadcast, but in the early days this was common. Now a broadcaster covers a team home and away, but before the nineteen-fifties, the away games were usually taken care of by re-creation. The announcer would sit in the studio and describe the game as the information was sent to him on the Western Union ticker.

One way to do this was to simply relay the information. Tom Hussey was the New England re-creation expert, and he employed the bare-bones method.

"Wally Berger at the plate." Tick, tick, tick, tick. "Strike one on Berger. Reds leading, 2 to 0." Tick, tick, tick, tick. "Berger flies out to Goodman in left."

But there was a more dramatic way, and many stations did this. They dressed the game up with sound effects—crowd noise, the bat hitting the ball, the background sounds of a vendor selling a hot dog.

Sometimes the dramatic method led to trouble. If the ticker broke down temporarily, the announcer could not simply say: "We are having trouble with the ticker." He had to improvise and, consequently, you would be treated to a batter hitting a dozen fouls in a row, or a sudden and inexplicable rain shower would appear until the ticker was repaired.

And the re-creation broadcaster sometimes painted himself into a corner. I remember one announcer who forgot there was a man on third. He had the batter flying deep to center field, with the outfielder making a sensational catch 420 feet from the plate.

But then the runner was thrown out trying to score from third. Obviously the fly ball had been an ordinary one, rather than a prodigious wallop. The announcer got out of this by having the runner fall down coming home and by having the centerfielder make one of the great throws in all of baseball history. (Turn up the crowd noise please, Mr. Engineer.)

I did a re-creation of the Boston University-Temple football game in 1951. The game was in Philadelphia and I was in the studios of WCOP in Boston. This was also the night of the Rocky Marciano-Jersey Joe Walcott heavyweight championship fight, which was being televised.

The Boston area always went wild over a Marciano fight, because the Rock was from nearby Brockton. I was no exception and the fact that there was a television set in the studio was too much of a temptation. Every time the fight would get interesting, I'd contrive to have a time out in the re-creation of the B.U.-Temple game.

"Let's go down to the field now and pick up the band," I'd say, and while some recorded music blared away, I'd catch some fight action.

This is not recommended as standard procedure for doing a re-creation.

Television entered the sports scene on May 17, 1939, when Bill Stern covered the Princeton-Columbia baseball game in New York City. Two weeks later, Lou Nova fought Max Baer, and announcer Sam Taub described the bout for what was, at best, a limited television audience.

That summer, Red Barber did a telecast of a doubleheader between the Dodgers and the Reds and that autumn the Fordham-Waynesburg football game was shown on TV.

The first telecast of a pro football game was also in the fall of 1939—between the Brooklyn Dodgers and the Philadelphia Eagles.

Telecasts of track meets and hockey games came shortly afterward. And on February 28, 1940, the Pitt-Fordham basketball game was televised from Madison Square Garden. It was the first ever on TV.

There were perhaps 300 sets in New York City in those days, and the reception had the look of a blizzard in Fairbanks. Even after the war, when television began to take giant strides, it took a while before the masses owned sets.

A Jimmy Breslin column describes a Bronx street scene on a hot summer's night in 1946, with men in their undershirts sitting outside a radio and appliance store staring at a pale blue light in the shop window. The light came from a seven-inch television set and on the mound for the Yankees was Frank "Specs" Shea, pitching New York to victory.

In those days, Breslin remembers, radio was still the thing, and when Mel Allen would go from one booth to another, it was the television booth that was the afterthought—a cramped room befitting its then status.

Now, the figures, both financial and otherwise, are staggering. Sports telecasting has become a multimillion-dollar industry. Indeed, there are critics who contend that it has become too big, that it rules the sporting world. Certainly the revenue from television contracts has kept franchises going and has contributed to the outsize salaries many of today's athletes receive.

Television has been criticized for such things as the scheduling of games at eleven in the morning on the West Coast so they'll be on TV in the East at a decent hour, two in the afternoon. The industry has been knocked for the compulsory time-outs so the network can sell beer or gasoline at thousands of dollars a commercial minute. Fans who

have braved miserable weather and paid eight bucks for a terrible seat fidget during these fake time-outs, while the warm customer at home takes another sip of his scotch and water and waits for the resumption of action.

There are two sides to that story. Pro football is the sport that gets criticized the most for commercial interruptions. True, the fan is inconvenienced slightly, but the commercials also make it possible for millions of others to see the game. I think it's safe to say that without television, pro football would not have made the strides it has in the last fifteen years. The fan at the game this week can see his team in Los Angeles next week—through the magic of television. The superfluous time-outs seem a small price to pay for this privilege.

I first covered pro football on television in 1954. There were two, sometimes three, cameras on the action then. Now there are mobile units, nine or ten cameras, miles of cables, slow motion, stop-action, instant replay, and even a color man on the field, interviewing the athletes as they come to the bench.

An early use of the isolated camera for a national football telecast was in the 1964 NFL championship game between the Browns and the Colts, which I covered. Millions were amazed as the camera followed Browns' receiver Gary Collins down the field and caught him grabbing one of his three touchdown passes.

On the second half kickoff in that game, I relayed a message to the television truck suggesting the director zoom in on number 44 on the kickoff team. He was a Cleveland rookie and often made the tackle on kickoffs. The camera isolated number 44 and, sure enough, he made the tackle. His name was Leroy Kelley, and he has gone on to be much more than a special team man for the Browns.

Fans think the instant replay is a mysterious technical maneuver, but it is a simple procedure. Each game is taped

in its entirety, and when a replay of a certain segment is wanted, that part of the tape is merely replayed at a signal from the director.

With the isolated camera, it is a matter of percentages and luck. A director must know who is likely to get the football on certain downs. If it is third and seven, a down-and-out pass is a distinct possibility, so you would follow the split receivers and possibly the tight end.

You might want to show the work of an offensive guard, and here it does not really matter what the play is. But if you follow the middle linebacker and he's not involved in the play, you simply don't show the isolation on replay.

The next sophistication of the television sports industry is apt to be a videotape recorder, so that if you're out of the house when a major event takes place, you can set the machine and watch the game at your convenience.

The broadcasting industry has come a long way from that Newark announcer with the match to today's split-screen-instant-replay-isolation-slow-motion-twenty-seven-inch-color-billion-dollar business.

Presumably, tomorrow's sports announcer will be better at his craft than the men who preceded him. But Tomorrow will have learned from Today, which in turn was taught by Yesterday.

CHAPTER 2

Baseball

I pulled out of the driveway that very pleasant October morning and headed for Boston. It was a typical New England autumn day, but for me, this one was different—the most exciting day of my professional life.

The September 28 telegram that led to all the excitement read this way:

PLEASED TO ADVISE THAT IN EVENT BOSTON PARTICI-
PATES IN 1967 WORLD SERIES YOU HAVE BEEN NOMINATED
AND APPROVED TO WORK ON THE TELECASTS OF GAMES
ONE, TWO, SIX, AND SEVEN IF NECESSARY. YOU WILL
SHARE THESE ASSIGNMENTS WITH CURT GOWDY ON TELE-
VISION AND PEEWEE REESE ON RADIO. YOUR CONTACT
WILL BE LOU KUSSEROW AT THE FENWAY COMMONWEALTH
HOTEL IN BOSTON AND THE GATEWAY HOTEL IN ST. LOUIS
WHERE WE HAVE MADE ARRANGEMENTS FOR YOU. WE
WOULD APPRECIATE YOUR CONFIRMING YOUR UNDER-
STANDING OF THESE ARRANGEMENTS.

CHET SIMMONS   NBC DIRECTOR OF SPORTS

So here it was. Twenty years after starting as a sports announcer in Rutland, Vermont, I was covering the World

Series. I had been edgy and nervous the night before but was calm when I arrived at Fenway Park.

Surprisingly, it had always been this way on major assignments. In the years of covering NFL championship games and the College All-Star Football Game the butter-flies were always there until I got to the field. Then the emotions fall away and my mind concentrates on the task at hand.

In the World Series I was to be introduced by Curt Gowdy, and as the home announcer I would give a descrip-tion of Fenway Park. I grew up in North Quincy, roughly seven miles from the ball park. I had sat in the centerfield bleachers and watched plenty of ball games as a boy, but it had taken much time and effort and many years of broad-casting to get to that booth and into a World Series.

Gowdy, ever the competent pro, sailed through the first four and a half innings. Then Curt turned the mike over, I took a deep breath, and there I was. Millions of people were watching, from all over America. Others have broad-cast a World Series game before and since, and I think it's accurate to say they probably had the same feeling I had in my first turn on play-by-play.

Even with a solid pro beside you and an excellent tech-nical crew, you are all alone. It is not unique, this feeling, and it ends quickly, but it is there for you as surely as it is for the player down on the field. Then you move into your groove and go about doing your job. The job is play-by-play baseball.

The listener may think the broadcaster arrives at the park a few minutes before game time, saunters into the booth, gets the engineer's signal, and starts talking. But as in most jobs, there is more to this than meets the eye or, in radio's case, the ear.

Even before you leave home there are preparations you

Excerpts
from the
Boston Red Sox
Press Book

BOSTON RED SOX

THOMAS A. YAWKEY
President

RICHARD H. O'CONNELL
Executive Vice-President
General Manager

JOHN ALEVIZOS
Vice-President, Administration

JOHN F. DONOVAN, JR.
Vice-President, Legal Affairs

HAYWOOD C. SULLIVAN
Vice-President, Player Personnel

JOSEPH T. CUMMISKEY
Treasurer

JOSEPH LaCOUR
Secretary

NEIL T. MAHONEY
Director, Player Procurement, Scouting

EDWARD F. KENNEY
Director, Minor League Clubs

JOHN J. ROGERS
Traveling Secretary

WILLIAM C. CROWLEY
Director of Public Relations

ARTHUR J. KEEFE
Statistician
Assistant Director of Public Relations

THOMAS B. DOWD
Community Relations, Speaking

EDWARD M. KASKO
Field Manager

INDEX

	Page
All-Star Players	44
American League	
All-Star Squad — 1971	47
Most Valuable Players	36
Standings, 1971	47
Statistics, 1971	26
Team Physicians	47
Attendance, 1971 Day by Day at Fenway	21
Attendance Information, Team and League	33
Batting	
All-Time Individual Records	42
All-Time Top Ten Red Sox Leaders	46
Individuals vs. Clubs, by months, home-away, vs.	
left-right, 1971	28, 29
League Champions, Red Sox	10
Red Sox With .300 Season Average	38
Team vs. Clubs, 1971	32
Year-by-Year Team Leaders	40
Day-by-Day Record, 1971	22, 23
Fenway Park Information	Inside front cover
Game-Winning RBIs, 1971	4
Gold Gloves, Red Sox	35
Grand Slams, current Red Sox career A.L. totals	20
Home Runs	
Individuals vs. Clubs, 1971	33
Individuals vs. Clubs, Lifetime	33
League Champions, Red Sox	6
Season, Red Sox With 20 or More	34
Hotels, Red Sox 1972	34
Hotels, Visiting Teams in 1972	34
Items of Interest	45
Manager and Coaching Staff	3
Minor League System	2
No-Hit Games, For and Against	37
Pinch Hitting, 1971	33
Pitching	
All-Time Individual Records	42
Individuals vs. Clubs, by Months, 1971	30, 31
Rival Pitchers' Records vs. Red Sox	36
Team vs. Clubs, 1971	32
Year-by-Year Team Leaders	41
Player Records	4-20
Public Relations Directory	Inside front cover
Radio, Television Network, 1972	44
Red Sox	
Club Leaders, 1971	35
Club Season Records	43
Miscellaneous Records, 1971	35
Record vs. Clubs, 1971	35
Roster, 1972	24, 25
Roster Changes, 1971	34
Runs Batted In, Red Sox Champions	9
Spring Training	
Schedule, 1972	Inside back cover
Sites	48
Statistics, 1971	48
Statistics, Complete 1971	27
Stolen Bases, Red Sox with 25 or more	37
Twenty-Game Winners	37
World Series, Red Sox results in	19
Year-by-Year Record	39

MINOR LEAGUE SYSTEM

EDWARD F. KENNEY, Director, Minor League Clubs
191 Liberty Street, Braintree, Mass. 02184

NEIL T. MAHONEY, Director, Player Procurement, Scouting
61 Thornton Road, Chestnut Hill, Mass. 02167

Pitching Instructor: BILL SLACK

Club (League)	Class	*Officials*
Louisville (International)		
Darrell Johnson, Manager	AAA	William A. Gardner, Pres.
Pawtucket (Eastern)		
Don Lock, Manager	AA	Neal Bennett, G.M.
Winston-Salem (Carolina)		
Rac Slider, Manager	A	Joseph J. Buzas, Pres.
Winter Haven (Florida State)		
John Butler, Manager	A	
Williamsport (New York-Penn)		
Dick Beradino, Manager	A	Joe Romano, Pres.

SCOUTS

Bolling, Milton J.
2752 Fontaine Bleau Drive, South
Mobile, Alabama 36606

Boone, Raymond O.
4950 Art Street
San Diego, Calif. 92115

Brown, Mace
305 N. Holden Road
Greensboro, N. C. 27410

Burns, Irving "Jack"
1185 Commonwealth Avenue
Brighton, Mass. 02135

DeLoof, Maurice
15680 Collingham Drive
Detroit, Mich. 48205

Digby, George
P.O. Box 865
Inverness, Fla. 32650

Doyle, Howard
1022 E. 3rd Street
Stillwater, Okla. 74074

Fahey, Frank
995 Grand Avenue
St. Paul, Minn. 55105

Johnson, Earl
9541 25th Avenue, N.W.
Seattle, Wash. 98107

Johnson, Stanley L.
56 Morningside Dr.
Daly City, Calif. 94015

Koney, Charles
509 Crandon Ave.
River Oaks Terrace
Calumet City, Ill. 60409

Lefebvre, Wilfrid "Lefty"
158 Greenfield Street
Seekonk, Mass. 02771

Maldonado, Felix J.
9 St. 652 Constancia
Ponce, Puerto Rico 00731

Malzone, Frank
16 Aletha Road
Needham, Mass. 02192

McCarey, C. J. "Socko"
822 Bellaire Avenue
Pittsburgh, Pa. 15226

Mele, Sabath A. "Sam"
340 Adams St.
Quincy, Mass. 02169

Nekola, F. J. "Bots"
13 Devonshire Drive
New Hyde Park, L.I., N.Y. 11040

Paffen, William
P.O. Box 3532
Caracas, Venezuela

Palmer, Meade
102 N. Linden Ave.
Hatboro, Pa. 19040

Philley, David
1336 E. Polk
Paris, Texas 75460

Ravish, Anthony
Simmons Plaza
Hudson, N.Y. 12534

Rice, Roderick B.
1309 Tarman Circle
Norman, Okla. 73069

Scott, Edward
472 E. Ridge Road
Mobile, Ala. 36617

Sczesny, Matthew
10-08 127th Street
College Point, L.I., N.Y. 11356

Stendel, Marvin B.
1220 Carol Ann Place
St. Louis, Mo. 63122

Stephenson, Joseph
822 Jade Way
Anaheim, Calif. 92805

Thomas, Alphonse "Tommy"
R.D. #1
Dallastown, Pa. 17313

Thomas, Larry Lee
3207 Demorest Road
Grove City, Ohio 43123

Wagner, Charles T.
1523 Linden Ave.
Reading, Pa. 19604

Wright, Glenn
638 E. Keats Avenue
Fresno, Calif. 93726

YASTRZEMSKI, Carl Michael (Yaz)　　OUTFIELDER

Born: Aug. 22, 1939, Southampton, L.I., N.Y. Ht.: 5'11"; Wt.: 182 lbs. Brown eyes, Brown hair. Bats: Left; Throws: Right. Home: Lynnfield, Mass. Signed by Scout Bots Nekola, Nov. 28, 1958. Married Carolann Casper. Children: Mary Ann 9/21/60, C. Michael Jr. 8/16/61, Suzann 6/15/66, Carolyn 4/15/69.

An 11-year veteran now, and one of baseball's superstars, Yaz is determined to come back from his poorest season of 1971. Hampered by a hand injury that never completely healed, he dropped off from his best season to his worst with the bat, but still won his sixth Gold Glove as the best left fielder in the game. He also set a major league record for outfielders as his 16 assists topped the A. L. in that category for an unprecedented sixth time.

A three-time batting champion and MVP in 1967 when he led the Red Sox to the "Impossible Dream" pennant, his 106 walks in 1971 were second only to Killebrew, and his 454 walks in the last four years are high for the league, another indicator of the respect he commands from rival pitchers.

An infielder in high school, Yaz signed with the Red Sox after his freshman year at Notre Dame, and later earned his degree from Merrimack College in Massachusetts. Despite his other off-season commitments as an associate in a Boston investing firm, director of a bank, and operating his own automobile dealership, he still found considerable time to spend on drug education work in schools in New England.

Year	Club	G	AB	R	H	2B	3B	HR	RBI	BA	BB	SO	E
1959	Raleigh	120	451	87	170*	34*	6	15	100	.377*	78	49	*45
1960	Minneapolis	148	570	84	193*	36	7	7	69	.339	47	65	5
1961	Boston	148	583	71	155	31	6	11	80	.266	50	96	10
1962	Boston	160	646	99	191	43	6	19	94	.296	66	82	*11
1963	Boston	151	570	91	183*	40	3	14	68	.321*	95	72	6
1964	Boston	151	567	77	164	29	9	15	67	.289	75	90	11
1965	Boston	133	494	78	154	45*	3	20	72	.312	70	58	3
1966	Boston	160	594	81	165	39*	2	16	80	.278	84	60	5
1967	Boston	161	579	112*	189*	31	4	44*	121*	.326*	91	69	7
1968	Boston	157	539	90	162	32	2	23	74	.301*	119	90	3
1969	Boston	162	603	96	154	28	2	40	111	.255	101	91	6
1970	Boston	161	566	125*	186	29	0	40	102	.329	128	66	14
1971	Boston	148	508	75	129	21	2	15	70	.254	106	60	2
Major Lg. Tot.		1692	6249	995	1832	368	39	257	939	.293	985	834	78

ALL-STAR GAME RECORD

Year	League	Pos.	AB	R	H	2B	3B	HR	RBI	BA	BB	SO	E
1963	American	OF	4	0	0	0	0	0	0	.000	0	2	0
1967	American	OF	4	0	3	1	0	0	0	.750	0	1	0
1968	American	OF	4	0	0	0	0	0	0	.000	0	2	0
1969	American	OF	1	0	0	0	0	0	0	.000	0	0	0
1970	American	OF-1B	6	1	4	1	0	0	0	.667	1	1	0
1971	American	OF	3	0	0	0	0	0	1	.000			
All-Star Game Tot.			20	1	7	2	0	0	1	.350	3	4	

Member of 1966 American League team but did not play.
Named to 1965 American League team but replaced due to injury.

WORLD SERIES RECORD

Year	Club	G	AB	R	H	2B	3B	HR	RBI	BA	BB	SO	E
1967	Boston	7	25	4	10	2	0	3	5	.400	4	1	0

TIANT, Luis Clemente (Luis)　　PITCHER

Born: November 23, 1940, Havana, Cuba. Ht.: 5'11"; Wt.: 190 lbs. Brown eyes, Black hair. Bats and Throws: Right. Home: Colonia Viaducto, Mex. Married Maria Del Refugio Navarro. Children: Luis, 9, Isabel, 4.

The 1971 season was certainly mixed up for Luis, a 21-game winner with a 1.60 ERA for Cleveland in 1968. He had a disappointing spring with Minnesota and was released. The Braves picked him up but he obtained his release from that organization after 30 days, and hooked on with Louisville. He showed enough there to be brought to Boston, where he had trouble as a starter because of early inning wildness, but showed a 1-1 record out of the bullpen and a 1.80 ERA. This winter he pitched a no-hitter in Venezuela and may be ready for a comeback as a long reliever.

Luis followed in the footsteps of his father who pitched for the New York Cuban professional team. He still holds the American League record for most strikeouts (19) in a 10-inning game, set in 1968.

Year	Club	G	GS	CG	W-L	IP	H	R	ER	BB	SO	ERA
1959	Mex. C. Tigers	41	27	11	5-19	184	214	139*	121	107	98	5.92
1960	Mex. C. Tigers	41	24	9	17-7	180	194	115	93	124*	107	4.65
1961	Mex. C. Tigers	24	19	10	12-9	145	138	77	61	106	141	3.78
1962	Jacksonville	1	0	0	0-0	1	0	0	0		1	0.00
1963	Charleston	29	20	4	7-8	139	141	75	56	72	99	3.63
1963	Burlington, N.C.	31	24	17	14-9	204	151	68	58	81	207*	2.56
1964	Portland	17	15	13	15-1	137	88	37	31	40	154	2.04
	Cleveland	19	16	9	10-4	127	94	41	40	47	105	2.83
1965	Cleveland	41	30	10	11-11	196	166	88	85	66	152	3.54
1966	Cleveland	46	16	9	12-11	155	121	50	48	50	145	2.79
1967	Cleveland	33	29	9	12-9	214	177	76	65	67	219	2.73
1968	Cleveland	34	32	19	21-9	258	152	53	46	73	264	1.60*
1969	Cleveland	38	37	9	9-20	250	229	123	129	129	156	3.71
1970	Minnesota-a	18	17	7	7-3	93	84	36	35	41	50	3.39
1971	Richmond-b-c	5	4	2	1-3	23	22	16	16	17	19	6.26
	Louisville	4	4	1	2-2	31	25	11	9	11	29	2.61
	Boston	21	10	1	1-7	72	73	42	39	32	59	4.88
Major Lg. Tot.		250	187	66	83-74	1365	1096	509	453	505	1150	2.99

a—Traded with pitcher Stan Williams to Minnesota Twins for pitchers Dean Chance and Bob Miller, outfielder Ted Uhlaender and outfielder-third baseman Graig Nettles, December 12, 1969.
b—On disabled list June 1 through August 3.
c—Unconditionally released by Twins March 31, 1971.
d—Released by Braves' organization May 15, 1971.

INDIVIDUAL SEASON RECORDS
BATTING

AT BATS
Left-handed, most .... 661, Roger Cramer, 1940
Right-handed, most .... 648, Dom DiMaggio, 1948
BASES ON BALLS, most .... 162, Ted Williams, 1947 & 1949
BATTING AVERAGE
Left-handed, highest .... .406, Ted Williams, 1941
Right-handed, highest .... .360, Jimmy Foxx, 1939
DOUBLES, most .... 67, Earl Webb, 1931
EXTRA BASES ON LONG HITS .... 201, Jimmy Foxx, 1938
GAMES, most .... 162, George Scott, 1966
.... 162, Carl Yastrzemski, 1969

GROUNDED INTO DOUBLE PLAYS
Left-handed, most .... 30‡, Carl Yastrzemski, 1964
Right-handed, most .... 32‡, Jackie Jensen, 1954
Fewest .... 3, Tony Lupien, 1943
HIT BY PITCHER, most .... 11, Ira Flagstead, 1924
HITS, most .... 222, Tris Speaker, 1912
most by rookie .... 205, Johnny Pesky, 1942
HITTING STREAKS, longest .... 34, Dom DiMaggio, 1949
longest start of season .... 20, Eddie Bressoud, 1964
HOME RUNS, most .... 50, Jimmy Foxx, 1938
at home .... 36, Jimmy Foxx, 1938
by position
    1b .... 50, Jimmy Foxx, 1938
    2b .... 27, Bobby Doerr, 1948 & 1950
    3b .... 28, Rico Petrocelli, 1971
    ss .... 40*, Rico Petrocelli, 1969
    lf .... 44, Carl Yastrzemski, 1967
    cf .... 25, Jackie Jensen, 1954
.... 25, Reggie Smith, 1969
    rf .... 36, Tony Conigliaro, 1970
    catcher .... 17, Bob Tillman, 1964
    pitcher .... 7, Wes Ferrell, 1935
grand slams .... 4, Babe Ruth, 1919
on road .... 19, Ted Williams, 1949
.... 19, Carl Yastrzemski, 1969
one month .... 14, Jackie Jensen, 1958
rookie .... 34, Walt Dropo, 1950
LONG HITS, most .... 92, Jimmy Foxx, 1938
RUNS, most .... 150, Ted Williams, 1949
RUNS BATTED IN, most .... 175, Jimmy Foxx, 1938
SACRIFICES
most, including flies .... 54, Jack Barry, 1917
most, no flies .... 35, Fred Parent, 1905
SINGLES, most .... 172, Johnny Pesky, 1947
SLUGGING PERCENTAGE
left-handed, highest .... .735, Ted Williams, 1941
right-handed, highest .... .704, Jimmy Foxx, 1938
STOLEN BASES, most .... 52, Tris Speaker, 1912
most caught stealing .... 19, Mike Menosky, 1920
STRIKE OUTS
left-handed, most .... 93, Carl Yastrzemski, 1964
right-handed, most .... 152, George Scott, 1966
fewest .... 9, Stuffy McInnis, 1921
TOTAL BASES, most .... 398, Jimmy Foxx, 1938
TRIPLES, most .... 22, Chick Stahl, 1904
.... 22, Tris Speaker, 1913

PITCHING

BASES ON BALLS
Left-hander, most .... 134, Mel Parnell, 1949
Right-hander, most .... 121, Don Schwall, 1962
EARNED RUNS, most .... 139, Jack Russell, 1930
EARNED RUN AVERAGE, lowest .... 1.01‡, Dutch Leonard (222 innings), 1914
GAMES, most .... 79, Dick Radatz, 1964
complete, most .... 41, Cy Young, 1902
finished, most .... 67‡, Dick Radatz, 1964
lost, most .... 25, Charley Ruffing, 1928
lost consecutively, most .... 12, Charley Ruffing, 1929
started, most .... 43, Cy Young, 1902
winning percentage, highest .... .872, Joe Wood (34-5), 1912
won, most .... 34, Joe Wood, 1912
won consecutively, most .... 16**, Joe Wood, 1912
HIT BATSMEN, most .... 20, Howard Ehmke, 1923
HITS, most .... 337, Cy Young, 1902
HOME RUNS, most .... 37, Earl Wilson, 1964
INNINGS, most .... 366, Cy Young, 1902
consecutive hitless, most .... 23, Cy Young, 1904
consecutive scoreless, most .... 45⅔, Cy Young, 1904
RUNS, most .... 162, Charley Ruffing, 1929
.... 162, Jack Russell, 1930

SHUTOUTS
Left-hander, most won .... 9*, Babe Ruth, 1916
Right-hander, most won .... 10, Cy Young, 1904
.... 10, Joe Wood, 1912
most lost .... 8, Joe Harris, 1906
won by 1-0, most .... 5**, Les Bush, 1918
STRIKE OUTS, most .... 258, Joe Wood, 1912
WILD PITCHES, most .... 21**, Earl Wilson, 1963

‡major league record;   *American League record;   **tied for league record

can make. Read the sports pages of every newspaper in town for valuable bits of information.

Pack your briefcase—yes, yes, by all means go purchase one—with the following helpmates:

- *The rule book,* which you should memorize.
- *The Baseball Register,* a *Sporting News* publication that provides background on every major leaguer.
- *Who's Who in Baseball,* available at most newsstands.
- *The Complete Handbook of Baseball,* which has scouting reports, predictions, team and player profiles.
- *The American League Red Book* and the *National League Green Book.*
- *The Little Red Book of Baseball,* which has records galore, ranging from most assists by a shortstop in a nine-inning game to the longest no-hitter.
- *Batting Averages at a Glance,* which can quickly update a hitter's average at any time during the game.

Each team in the league provides a press book, which has biographies on each player and much more. Obviously you can't memorize the book but you should be familiar enough with it so you can quickly find what you are looking for.

Anyone who speaks for a living can tell you that some of the best ad libs are written. Frequently I'll gather notes on players from magazines or newspaper articles. It is important to read as much as you can about the men who play the game.

You should get to the park early, and make it a point to talk to the managers. If they aren't available, consult a coach or a trainer to find out if everybody is on hand and ready to play. If a player is not in the lineup and you don't know why, you are not doing your job.

Spend as much time as you can in the dugouts and around the batting cage. This is a time when the players are free and easy. There is plenty of banter and small talk, so you may pick up some valuable information.

Don't be afraid to ask questions. You'll never know unless you ask. You can find out, if a team is in for the first game of a series, who is hot with the bat, who is in a slump, what a rookie pitcher likes to throw, a funny thing that happened last week.

Obviously the more you know about a player, the more you can use about him on the air.

Of course you can't talk to every player. Sometimes there are team meetings, sometimes pitchers are running in the outfield, others are wrapped up in their own preparation for the game, and some just don't want to talk.

The first year I covered major league baseball, in 1954 with the Cleveland Indians, one of the star pitchers was Early Wynn, who nearly twenty years later was elected to the Hall of Fame. I learned quickly that you did not speak to Early on the day he was pitching. A very nice guy on other days, he would sit silently in the dugout, building the emotional fire that made him the great competitor he was. I've met no one quite like Early in this respect, but as a general rule I don't bother a pitcher the day he is starting. Most of them don't care much for small talk.

There is always the exception, such as Fritz Peterson of the Yankees. Fritz is a professor at Northern Illinois, and one of his subjects is pocket billiards. Shooting pool is one of my hobbies and we often talk about it.

As in any line of work, common sense is king. Gather your information in a quiet, unobtrusive way, so that the player or manager isn't saying to himself, "Here he comes again." The last thing I do before going upstairs is to jot down the lineups posted in each dugout.

Now let's go up to the broadcasting booth.

The first move there is to make up my scorecard for the game. I make it a point in preparing it to put down beside the name of each player his home runs, his RBI's and batting average, and *always* make reference to them the first time he comes to bat. This information is provided by each club on a statistical sheet. Having these figures on the scorecard also helps if a player hits a home run. A quick glance at the card makes it possible for you to say, "That was number fifteen for Bobby Murcer." I also write down the pitcher's won-and-lost record and his earned run average.

The broadcaster must score the game as it progresses, and almost everyone I know has his own method. You should score the way that is easiest for you without distracting from your concentration on the game.

It is extremely important to note that radio and television are completely different media. Right now let's do a game on radio between the Red Sox and the Yankees at Yankee Stadium in New York.

In recent years our broadcasting crew for the Red Sox has consisted of Ned Martin, Johnny Pesky, me, and our engineer, Al Walker.

As chief announcer on the crew I will do the first three innings, Ned will work the middle three, and I will finish up the game. Pesky, a former major league shortstop and manager, will do the "color," providing insights that come from his having spent many years on the field.

Three microphones are set up, with Ned on my left and Johnny on the right. Al Walker, situated behind us, has called the station in Boston and will give us a cue. Sometimes this is done merely by pointing to the announcer. In our case Al has a small light, which is in front of me, and which will flash on when we take the air. With thirty seconds to go Al will say, "Stand by." We will then sit silently waiting for the go-ahead sign.

Martin starts the broadcast by setting the stage. He will

mention the weather, give the dimensions of the ball park and the records of the pitchers, and run down the starting lineups. He will cover the umpiring assignments and, if time allows, may talk about who is injured or sick and will not play, the standings of the teams, how they have fared against each other in the past, etc. He will be prepared to stop when the public address announcer invites the fans to stand for the national anthem. Ned will carry on until it is time for the first pitch. As the catcher throws the ball down to second he will say, "Now, for the play-by-play, here is Ken Coleman."

COLEMAN: Thank you, Ned, and good evening, everyone. Tommy Harper will lead off for the Red Sox. The speedy right-handed batter steps in to face veteran right-handed Mel Stottlemyre. Stottlemyre, the tall, rangy right-hander, winds and throws and the first pitch to Harper is over at the knees for a called strike. Third baseman Rich McKinney, acquired from the White Sox in an off-season deal, is playing up the line on Harper. He is well aware of Tommy's speed and the possibility that he may try to bunt his way on. The 0 to 1 pitch is a curve ball outside and low and the count is one and one.

(*Note that you give the count between each pitch and you give the balls ahead of the strikes. On radio you establish that the batter bats right- or left-handed and the pitcher is a lefty or a righty.*)

COLEMAN: Harper is batting .265 at the moment, with nine home runs and twenty-three runs batted in. In 1969 Tommy stole seventy-three bases, the most in the American League since Ty Cobb stole ninety-six in 1915. The one-one pitch is hammered sharply toward short. Gene Michael moves quickly to his left, comes up with it, and throws on to first and Harper is out.

PESKY: Harper hit a sinking fast ball around the knees

and we can expect that we'll see a lot of ground balls if Stottlemyre has his stuff today. He is most effective when he keeps the ball down.

COLEMAN: Luis Aparicio steps in on the right side. The veteran shortshop, now in his seventeenth year, is hitting .270 with four homers and thirty-two runs batted in. He stands deep in the box with a slightly closed stance and his feet fairly close together.

(*The term "closed stance" is understood by the knowledgeable baseball fan. Occasionally you can explain the meaning, which is that the batter has his front foot closer to the plate than his back foot as he stands in the batter's box.*)

COLEMAN: The pitch to Aparicio is swung on and lined toward left center. Roy White and Bobby Murcer are running hard—it goes between them for a base hit, Aparicio rounds first and is heading for second. White comes up with the ball and fires it in, Aparicio slides and he is safe with a double.

PESKY: White made a good play on that ball, cutting it off and coming up with a strong throw to Horace Clarke, the second baseman, but Aparicio just beat the ball to the bag. If that ball had gone by White it would have been trouble for New York because there's a lot of ground out there and Luis might have wound up on third.

COLEMAN: So the Red Sox here in the first inning have a runner on second with one down and the batter is Carl Yastrzemski. Carl is batting .291 with twenty-two homers and fifty-one runs batted in as he has bounced back well from an off-season last year. The left-handed batter stands deep in the box and cocks the bat high behind his left shoulder. Stottlemyre, working deliberately, now goes into his stretch, looks toward second, turns, and throws, and Yaz slices a foul ball into the seats in back of third for strike one.

PESKY: Ken, one thing that Carl is doing this year is going to left field with the outside pitch. That's the way he batted in his great years and I'm glad to see him back to it. It's tough to try and pull that outside pitch. That time he was just trying to meet the ball and drive it into left field.

COLEMAN: Right, John, and in this ball park with that short porch in right, Mel is going to try to pitch him down and away.

(*Note here that we referred to each other by name. This is permissible occasionally but shouldn't be done every time there is an exchange.*)

COLEMAN: Stottlemyre swings into action and throws— there's a line drive deep into right field, Callison goes back toward the fence . . . *but it's gone for a home run, deep into the lower stands in right and the Red Sox take a two-to-nothing lead on Carl Yastrzemski's twenty-third home run of the year.*

Let's suppose that we were doing the same segment of a game on television. On radio it was our job to paint the word pictures. On TV the picture is already there. The announcer must realize that he subordinates his effort to complete what the fan at home is already seeing. You will have a monitor in front of you, a small TV set that shows you the same picture the viewer has in his living room. There is no need to state that the pitcher is winding up, etc., because the viewer can see this for himself.

You would give the background information just as you would on radio but you also will be following the monitor. The home runs, RBI's, and batting average will be flashed on the screen, and you can simply repeat them or you can say: "Here are the figures on Harper." On the ground ball he hit to Michael, it would suffice to say, "Michael—to Ellis—one out."

Often what you say on TV will be dictated by what the director is showing on the screen. You will be wearing earphones and the director will lead you into what he is going to show. For example, after the first pitch to Harper it would be common practice for the director to say over the earphone, "On deck." This means he will be showing the player on deck, so when the shot comes up you can say, "There's Aparicio, who will bat next." In the reference I made to McKinney on radio I would do the same on TV, particularly if the camera does not show where McKinney is. On TV you can involve yourself more with background information on the players because you are not involved in description.

It has been my experience that television is tougher to do than radio because between each pitch, as opposed to the free flow of words on radio, you are involved in making a decision. Do I have something to say? Is it *really* worth saying? Is it pertinent? Too much talk on TV annoys the viewer, perhaps more in baseball than in any other sport, and it is a delicate area.

I've given you the picture of what it is like on the major league level and the many tools you will have to work with. But what about you on your first job in a small local station? On Thursday afternoon the station manager informs you that you will be doing the local high school baseball game on Saturday. The team is playing in the state tournament and you will cover the game on radio. There are no press books, guides, or other literature on the teams. You'll be working on a card table set up behind the screen at home plate with fans all around you. The visiting team will arrive by bus a couple of hours before the game. How do *you* prepare?

On Friday you get the coaches on the phone and write down as much information as they can give you on each player. In other words, you take a cram course. Possibly the boss will give you Friday afternoon off so you can watch the home team in practice. You simply have to dig in and bear down and get all the facts you can by yourself. You are being thrown into the pool and you are expected to swim.

Before you ever got this first job, though, when you first became interested in sports announcing, you practiced. How? Well, for one thing you went to local sandlot games and did the play-by-play in your head. At home you had listened to the major league broadcasters and subconsciously picked up techniques of delivery. You bought a tape recorder and turned the sound down on the TV set and practiced doing games, using both a radio and a TV-type delivery. You learned all you could about the game itself. Quite possibly you played some baseball as a boy growing up.

How are you going to do the game? What is your style? Your technique? Are you going to do it like Ken Coleman or Curt Gowdy or Vin Scully or Lindsey Nelson or Ernie Harwell or Harry Caray?

The answer is that you are going to do it a little bit like all the announcers you have heard, but mostly you are going to do it the way that comes naturally to you. Like fingerprints, there are no two announcers exactly alike. It is something akin to the ballplayer at bat. You get the stance that is comfortable for you so you can be as productive as possible. There are men who can coach you and critique you, but finally you are going to have to come to terms with yourself.

Mel Allen on radio years ago was a good example of the rapid-fire dramatic delivery. Red Barber, on the other hand, was a low-key man with a flair for understatement. They were both excellent broadcasters but used different techniques.

Some announcers are out-and-out "homers." They root

for the home team. Jack Brickhouse in Chicago has been heard to say, with Ron Santo at bat for the Cubs, "Come on, Ronnie, let's get a hold of one." Bob Prince, the voice of the Pirates, will say when the game is over, "We had 'em all the way."

Others will be more objective. Ernie Harwell in Detroit works right down the middle on his broadcasts. They are all pros and are all good at it, but they are all different.

A word here about official scoring. Broadcasters get the scorer's decision either through a squawk box from the press row or by hand signals from up there. The temptation is to second-guess the decision, or even to first-guess it —that is, say something like: "Well, that can't be anything but an error."

I try to avoid this sort of thing. Second-guessing takes no great talent. Anyone can do it. Not only that, the scorer is an official of the league and his decisions should be treated with the same respect in the broadcaster's booth as those of an umpire.

You might as well know right now that no sports announcer—particularly a baseball announcer, because he is on the air so often for so many months—pleases everybody. I've received complimentary and caustic mail on the same day about the same game. So have all the others. It is part of the business and you will have to learn to live with the criticism as well as the praise and keep your feet on the ground.

Whatever your technique, there are some rules we must all follow:

• Give the score early and often.
• Never say the score is "three to two"—it is always "Boston three, New York two." Just three to two doesn't mean anything to the person who just tuned in.
• Keep your eye on the ball. Don't get caught looking at

your scorecard before a catch is made in the outfield. Sometimes the ball is dropped and you, as well as the outfielders, are in trouble.

• At the end of each half inning as the team takes the field, look to see if any substitutions are made.

In this same area there are some general, rather flexible rules to follow. Two main factors in being a successful broadcaster on either radio or TV in baseball are believability and wearability. You must always strive to tell it like it is. If you make a mistake and know it, you should correct it immediately. If your partner catches it he should call it to your attention. There is no harm in poking a little fun at yourself when this happens.

One night in Kansas City some years ago Rocky Colavito was playing right field for Cleveland. In describing his efforts to catch a fly ball I intended to say, "There goes Rocky back against the wall." Instead it came out, "There goes Wally back against the Rock." I caught the fluff and said, "For those of you interested in statistics, that was my twelfth fluff of the year, which puts me in third place in the American League." Apparently it took me off the hook because the mail indicated that people got a kick out of it.

As far as wearability is concerned, remember that in baseball you are a visitor in someone's home for several hours a day for about seven months of the year, counting spring training games. Hopefully you are a welcome guest. I don't think you can make every game sound like the seventh game of the World Series. If it is a very exciting game you will get caught up in the drama and should give it all you've got. You will have a percentage of games that are simply not exciting. These are the toughest to do. Do what you can to make them interesting but don't try to con the fan. He or she is too knowledgeable to be taken in by false enthusiasm. This doesn't mean that because the game is dull you have to be dull too. It is simply a matter of being honest.

Who does the baseball announcer work for?

Basically the announcer works for the fan. In some cities he is hired by the baseball club, in others by the station, and in still others by the advertising agency that represents the sponsor. Generally, the team, while it may not make the selection, will have the choice of final approval. In the many years I have been broadcasting I have never been told by an official of a team what to say regarding play-by-play work. Teams do have places during each game in which promotional announcements are scheduled, and they will provide you with the copy.

Earlier I discussed the different styles or techniques of various broadcasters. I have always taken the position that the job of the play-by-play man is to *report* the action on the field. He is not hired to manage, to second-guess, or to comment on the validity of the moves. He should give credit where it is due on both sides. It is inevitable in baseball reporting, when you cover one team all season long, that your personal feelings will come to the surface occasionally. A fellow would have to be a pretty cold fish to live and work with a team, to get to know the executives, the manager, the coaches, and the players and not want to see them win.

It is, of course, a great deal more fun when the team comes out on top. In 1966 the Red Sox finished half a game out of tenth place. In 1967 they came out of nowhere to win the American League pennant with a driving finish over the second half of the season. The entire New England area was caught up in the race as an epidemic of pennant fever broke out. Even nonbaseball fans were swept up in the excitement of the Red Sox's dramatic effort.

It may seem like a strange analogy, but I have found that the baseball broadcaster's life is not unlike that of the players. There are times when you feel right on top of things and times when you go into slumps. You should strive, as the player does, for consistency. If you have what you think is a bad day at the microphone, you can't dwell on it. Instead, you have to bounce back the next day with your best effort.

The baseball broadcaster has a tough and demanding role that requires a good deal of self-discipline. It is important to get your rest and be prepared to do your job. You have a responsibility to your listeners, to your employer, to your sponsors, to your family, and to yourself.

CHAPTER 3

Football

There we were, Frank Gifford and I, dressed like a couple of Admiral Byrd's North Pole explorers that cold, snowy morning of January 2, 1966.

We were standing in front of the Northland Hotel in Green Bay, Wisconsin, at 8:30 A.M., waiting for a cab to take us to the stadium, where that afternoon the Packers and the Cleveland Browns would tangle for the championship of the National Football League.

We had to be at the park early to "cut the billboards" for the game, a billboard being that spot at the opening and closing of a telecast when the announcer says, "Today's game is brought to you by . . ." and then lists the sponsors.

As the cab crawled along in the storm the memories stirred. The first professional football game I had ever done had been in the rickety old stadium they had in Green Bay in 1952.

That was the beginning of a fourteen-year association with the Cleveland Browns. It is good to broadcast for any pro team but especially nice to work for a winner. For most of those years, the Browns were winners.

Frank and I met that morning with Howard Reifsnyder, our producer, and finished our early work. Ray Scott would join us around 11:30 for final discussion of the game. Ray

I'm centering for the Cleveland Browns. Milt Plum is quarterback, and for running mates I have Bobby Mitchell (49) and Jim Brown (32). *Photo by Warren (Ohio)* Tribune

was to work the first half play-by-play. I would do the second half and Frank would handle the color assignment and comment on the instant replays.

We walked down through the empty stands at about 10:15 and into the locker rooms. The Browns, who had stayed overnight in Appleton, Wisconsin, were not on the scene yet, so we went into the Packers' room.

I'll never forget Vince Lombardi's performance there. I didn't know Lombardi well. I'd met him a few times at N.F.L. meetings, but not for long enough to establish a rapport. I knew his reputation, of course, as a stern disciplinarian and taskmaster, but he didn't act the part that morning.

As the Green Bay players trooped in, they were met by a different Lombardi. This one chewed nobody out, made no sarcastic remarks, brought up no previous game mistakes. He smiled, joked, kidded around with his players—a Lombardi the public seldom heard about, but a reason why he was a great coach.

His work in getting ready for the championship game was done. The preparations had been made and now the game belonged to the men on the field. Lombardi's job now, knowing the built-in tensions that come with playing for a title, was to have his players as loose and ready as possible so they would function at their best.

They knew what was at stake. They were emotionally ready and he didn't want them wound too tight. Like a master chef mixing a salad, he wanted the ingredients just right. With Lombardi, they usually were.

The Packers won that game, 23 to 12, on the sloppy field. The tedious preparations had paid off.

Football coaches work long, hard hours. So do announcers. More than in any other sport, the football broadcaster must do his homework. If you haven't prepared yourself during the week you are in trouble. You will be no

CLEVELAND BROWNS - 11/1/64
NUMERICAL ROSTER

No.	Name	Pos.	Ht. - Wt.	Yr.	School
11	Ninowski, Jim	QB	6.1--207	7	Michigan State
13	Ryan, Frank	QB	6.3--200	7	Rice
20	Fichtner, Ross	DB	6.0--185	5	Purdue
22	Caylor, Lowell	DB	6.3--205	1	Miami (Ohio)
23	Benz, Larry	DB	5.11-185	2	Northwestern
24	Franklin, Bobby	DB	5.11-182	5	Mississippi
26	Raimey, Dave	DB	5.10-195	1	Michigan
27	Roberts, Walter	FL	5.10-175	1	San Jose State
30	Parrish, Bernie	DB	5.11-195	6	Florida
32	Brown, Jim	FB	6.2--228	8	Syracuse
35	Fiss, Galen	LB	6.0--227	9	Kansas
36	Scales, Charley	FB	5.11-215	5	Indiana
38	Sczurek, Stan	LB	5.11-230	2	Purdue
42	Warfield, Paul	FL	6.0--188	1	Ohio State
44	Kelly, Leroy	HB	6.0--195	1	Morgan State
48	Green, Ernie	HB	6.2--205	3	Louisville
49	Beach, Walter	DB	6.0--185	2	Central Michigan
50	Costello, Vince	LB	6.0--228	8	Ohio Univ.
52	Lucci, Mike	LB	6.2--223	3	Tennessee
56	Morrow, John	C	6.3--248	8	Michigan
60	Wooten, John	G	6.3--250	6	Colorado
62	Memmelaar, Dale	G	6.2--248	6	Wyoming
66	Hickerson, Gene	G	6.3--248	7	Mississippi
67	Williams, Sidney	DE	6.2--235	1	Southern Univ.
69	Kanicki, Jim	DT	6.4--270	2	Michigan State
70	Brown, John	T	6.2--248	3	Syracuse
72	Bundra, Mike	DT	6.4--260	3	U.S.C.
73	Clark, Monte	T-C	6.6--265	6	U.S.C.
74	Modzelewski, Dick	DT	6.0--260	12	Maryland
75	Shoals, Roger	T	6.4--255	2	Maryland
76	Groza, Lou	K	6.3--250	14	Ohio State
77	Schafrath, Dick	T	6.3--255	6	Ohio State
78	Parker, Frank	DT	6.5--255	3	Oklahoma State
80	Glass, Bill	DE	6.5--255	7	Baylor
82	Houston, Jim	LB	6.3--240	5	Ohio State
83	Brewer, John	E	6.4--235	4	Mississippi
84	Wiggin, Paul	DE	6.3--245	8	Stanford
85	McNeil, Clifton	FL	6.2--185	1	Grambling
86	Collins, Gary	FL	6.4--208	3	Maryland
87	Hutchinson, Tom	E	6.1--190	2	Kentucky

The numerical roster is invaluable.

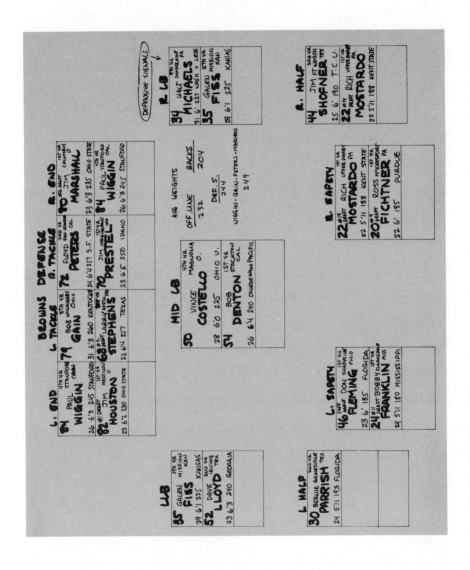

The defensive chart is on one side of a board, the offensive on the other—for quick flipping and identification.

BROWNS OFFENSE

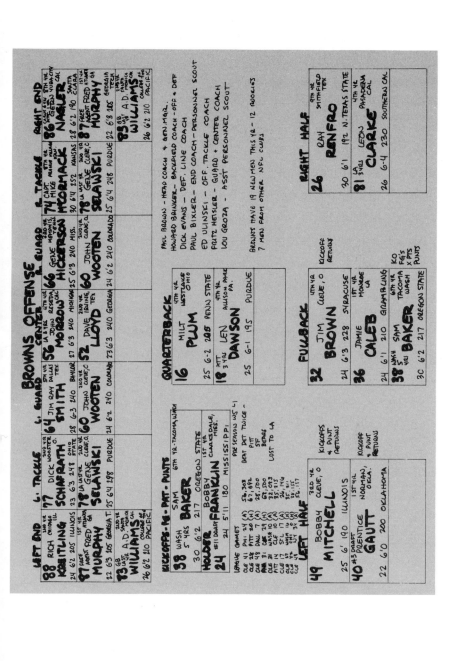

LEFT END	L. TACKLE	L. GUARD	CENTER	R. GUARD	R. TACKLE	RIGHT END
88 KREITLING RICH — 2ND YR, C. ONTONIO ILL, ILLINOIS — 24 6'2 205 ILLINOIS	**77 SCHAFRATH** DICK — 2ND YR, WOOSTER O., OHIO STATE — 23 6'3 248 OHIO STATE	**64 SMITH** JIM RAY — 5TH YR, DALLAS TEX, BAYLOR — 28 6'3 240 BAYLOR	**56 MORROW** JOHN — 4TH YR, RESEDA CAL, MICHIGAN — 27 6'3 240 MICHIGAN	**66 HICKERSON** GENE — 4TH YR, MEMPHIS, MISS — 25 6'3 240 MISS.	**74 CAPT McCORMACK** MIKE — 8TH YR, KANSAS CITY — 30 6'4 252 KANSAS	**86 NAGLER** MIKE — 5TH YR, CALGARY, YUBA CITY CAL — 28 6'2 190 SANTA CLARA
87 MURPHY FRED — 1ST YR, FREE AGENT, ATLANTA GA — 22 6'3 205 GEORGIA T.	**78 SELAWSKI** GENE — 1ST YR, LA CASTYL CLEVE O. — 25 6'4 298 PURDUE	**60 WOOTEN** JOHN — 2ND YR, CLEVE O. — 24 6'2 240 COLORADO	**52 LLOYD** DAVE — 2ND YR, IRVING TEX — 23 6'3 240 GEORGIA	**60 WOOTEN** JOHN — 2ND YR, CLEVE O. — 24 6'2 240 COLORADO	**78 SELAWSKI** GENE — 2ND YR, LA LAST YR CLEVE O. — 25 6'4 298 PURDUE	**87 MURPHY** FRED — 1ST YR, FREE AGENT, ATLANTA GA — 22 6'3 205 GEORGIA TECH
73 WILLIAMS A.D. — 2ND YR, SANTA MONICA CAL, COLLEGE of PACIFIC — 26 6'2 210 PACIFIC						**73 WILLIAMS** A.D. — 2ND YR, SANTA MONICA CAL, COLLEGE of PACIFIC — 26 6'2 210 PACIFIC

QUARTERBACK
16	**PLUM** MILT — 4TH YR, WESTLAKE OHIO, PENN STATE	25 6'2 205 PENN STATE
18	**DAWSON** LEN — 4TH YR, ALLISON PA., PITT	25 6'1 195 PURDUE

FULLBACK
32	**BROWN** JIM — 4TH YR, CLEVE O., SYRACUSE	24 6'3 228 SYRACUSE
36	**CALEB** JAMIE — 1ST YR, MONROE LA, GRAMBLING	24 6'1 210 GRAMBLING
38	**BAKER** SAM — 6TH YR, WASH, TACOMA WASH	30 6'2 217 OREGON STATE — KO, FG's, X PTS, PUNTS

KICKOFFS - FG - PAT - PUNTS
38	**BAKER** SAM — 5 YRS, WASH, TACOMA WASH	30 6'2 217 OREGON STATE
24	**FRANKLIN** BOBBY — 1ST YR, 1ST DRAFT, CLARKSDALE, MISS.	24 5'11 180 MISSISSIPPI — KICKOFF + PUNT RETURNS

LEFT HALF
49	**MITCHELL** BOBBY — 3RD YR, CLEVE O., ILLINOIS	25 6'0 190 ILLINOIS — KICKOFFS + PUNT RETURNS
40 #3 DRAFT	**GAUTT** PRENTICE — 1ST YR, NORMAN, OKLA, OKLAHOMA	22 6'0 200 OKLAHOMA — KICKOFF + PUNT RETURNS

RIGHT HALF
26	**RENFRO** RAY — 4TH YR, SMITHFIELD TEX, N. TEXAS STATE	30 6'1 192 N. TEXAS STATE
81	**CLARKE** LEON — 4TH YR, LA PASADENA CAL, SOUTHERN CAL	26 6'4 230 SOUTHERN CAL

PAUL BROWN - HEAD COACH + GEN. MGR.
HOWARD BRINKER - BACKFIELD COACH - OFF + DEF
DICK EVANS - DEF. LINE COACH
PAUL BIXLER - END COACH - PERSONNEL SCOUT
ED ULINSKI - OFF. TACKLE COACH
FRITZ HEISLER - GUARD + CENTER COACH
LOU GROZA - ASST PERSONNEL SCOUT

BROWNS HAVE 19 NEW MEN THIS YR - 12 ROOKIES
7 MEN FROM OTHER NFL CLUBS

better than the amount of preparation you bring into the booth Saturday or Sunday afternoon.

Each team will provide you with a press book similar to the one described in the baseball chapter. The N.F.L. sends out weekly statistical sheets, feature stories, and other material, such as upcoming schedules and who's injured. You will get a numerical roster from the publicity directors of teams on the pro and college levels. This is commonly referred to as the "three deep." It lists the players by position, going down to the third string, and includes numbers, height, weight, year in school, high school, hometown. From this material you will make up a "spotting board."

Every broadcaster has his own idea of what a spotting board should be. I use a magnetic board with the offense on one side, the defense on the other, and a separate numerical roster (I call this a panic sheet). The numerical roster is especially helpful on coverage of "special teams," such as kickoff and punt return units.

You may want to use my board or devise one of your own that's more comfortable for you. In any event, get the information and make the board as early in the week as possible. When you've finished, the board becomes your companion. Even as you shave in the morning, you might glance at the names and the numbers. When you're driving and stop at a red light, study it. By the end of the week you *know* that board.

Read about the teams you are going to cover, and if you can, go out and watch them practice. Jot notes about players on a yellow legal pad and have it with you at game time.

As in all other sports, it is essential to know the rules. I've always made it a point at the beginning of each season to review the rule book, and I find it helpful to write out in longhand specific situations, using team names. If you've ever seen a rule book with references to team A and team B you will see why it helps to simplify the method by naming teams and players instead of puzzling over A-1 and B-2.

During the week, if possible, you should look at films of the teams involved in the upcoming game. This will help you to find out what formations a team uses and you can study the line play.

Unlike the coach, however, you are most interested in the use of film for the purpose of identification. You must be able to quickly and accurately name the players in the game and should concentrate on this area when you are looking at film.

In addition to your own preparation, you will need two men who will work for you as spotters. Generally the team will provide you with a man. Sometimes he is an injured player, sometimes just a rabid fan, but in any case he must know the personnel on the team. Ideally you will have permanent spotters to work with you each week. On the pro level I worked for years with just one man, John Wellman, who would spot the team playing the Browns.

If possible you will get the spotting board to him a day or so before the game. If not, he must be in the booth at least an hour before game time to study your board. He may see who makes the play on the field, but if he can't point the name out on the board he is not helping you. There is a knack to spotting, and you can help a man do a good job by explaining to him that he must anticipate situations.

When his team has the ball he must point to the ball carrier. When his team is on defense he should follow the flow of the play from the defensive side so he can identify the tackler. When his team is going to receive a punt he must point to the deep men. But he must also be alert for the possibility of someone blocking a punt. He should always be looking for interceptions when the opposing team passes. He should point out good blocks by the offensive line.

You may be asking why he does all this when you yourself have memorized the teams. The answer is that hopefully you will be able to spot most of the things yourself, but you need all the extra sets of eyes you can get in the booth, and he is there to aid you.

It is important to point out to a spotter, if it is his first assignment—which is often the case—that he should not get rattled if he has trouble early in the game. He should not let his mistakes bother him. You'll know very quickly whether he is doing his job. If he is, it gives you a relaxed feeling. If he isn't, then your own homework will have paid off even more. Not getting rattled also applies to the broadcaster and could fit into any chapter in this book. In anything that you do on the air you must not allow yourself the luxury of dwelling on your mistakes. As long as you are a broadcaster you will make them. You cannot let this spoil your concentration.

Let me illustrate. I had had a particularly busy week, taping some bowling shows before going to Dallas for a big Browns-Cowboys game that was being carried on the full CBS network. Early in the contest I said the ball was on the twenty-seven-yard line instead of the twenty-two. Ordinarily I would have shaken this off and rolled right along. Perhaps because of the culmination of the work week, I was tired. In any event, I had to really fight myself to get back into the groove. Fortunately it was a personal thing, something that you think about yourself but which is not obvious to the listener, so I struggled through.

It is pointless to amplify mistakes in your mind to the point where you really might be affected in your delivery. You are a pro, and this is why you should reassure the spotter so that he doesn't fall apart on you during the game.

In addition to the two spotters, you will also have a statistician. He will keep track of the first downs, pass attempts and completions, distance on punts (always figured from the line of scrimmage), individual runners, individual pass receivers, etc. Sometimes, especially in high school ball, he will also be your color man. The most important matter to work out with him is communication. His information is no good unless he gets it to you. On first down, the way I work it, the statistician has a small pad of paper with a number on each page, say from one to thirty, like a daily calendar. When the initial first down is made he simply rips off the first sheet—with the number on it—and throws it in front of me. He continues to do this throughout the game.

Announcers generally have a good idea of their own strengths and weaknesses. One of my weaknesses is arithmetic. When a runner goes from his own thirty-eight to the opposing twenty-nine-yard line, it is difficult for me to add while talking, so the statistician does the arithmetic for me and hands me a slip of paper with "33" written on it. Immediately I can say, "Brown just ran for thirty-three yards."

I remember a game in Washington when Jim Brown and Bobby Mitchell were the Cleveland running backs. Brown had twice rushed for 237 yards in a game, the N.F.L. record, but in this game Mitchell had already chalked up 232 early in the fourth quarter. Cleveland had a big lead, however, and Bobby was taken out. If Paul Brown had somehow been able to hear us, I know he would have left Mitchell in. He had no way of knowing how close Mitchell was to the record. Mitchell had not only earned the chance, but knowing Paul Brown, I'd say that he would have liked setting up a new target for Jim Brown. Anyway, Mitchell never got to break the record.

As for Jim, we always kept individual figures on him. You never knew when he would break his or somebody

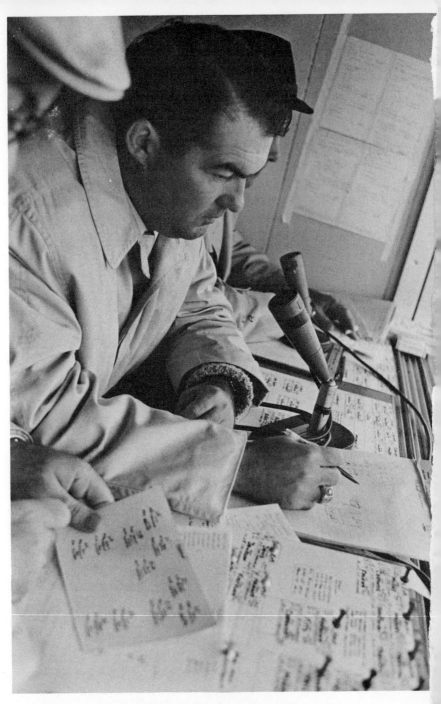

On the job at Cleveland's Municipal Stadium.
Photo by Beacon (Ohio) Journal

else's record. In any event, the statistician, like the spotter, is vital.

The color man is an important part of football, and I've enjoyed working with some of the best, such as Frank Gifford, Pat Summerall, and Tom Brookshier. It is important that you work as a team. My philosophy has always been, and I have always made it clear to any color man I've worked with, that the mike is just as much his as it is mine and he should feel free to pop in at any time. The good ones are sharp enough to come in only when there is something pertinent to say in analyzing the game.

My first experience in broadcasting football was typical of the way many start. I did high school games on WJDA in Quincy, Massachusetts, covering the South Shore of Boston, where I grew up.

High school football is the toughest. The broadcasting facilities are not always adequate. The ideal situation has you perched high over the action in the middle of the field. In high school you may be standing on an orange crate in the end zone. You are usually a staff announcer doing all kinds of other shows and don't have the time to prepare the way you do when you are strictly a sportscaster. Often you are doing a game between teams you haven't seen.

College football is not as difficult. By this time in your career you probably have more time to prepare. Generally you cover one team on a regular basis. I have done Boston University, Ohio State, and Harvard football and it is exciting work.

Pro football is the easiest. Professional rosters do not change as much as the high school or college ones, and you practically live with the team. When I reported to the Browns in 1952 I was fortunate because coach Paul Brown, a very thorough man, insisted that I spend all my time at the training camp with the players. I lived in a room on the Hiram College campus, where the team trained. It was

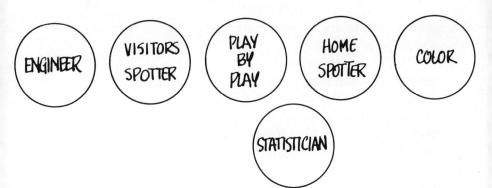

Here's how we normally line up in the broadcast booth.

Paul's idea that if I was going to broadcast Cleveland Browns football I should learn all there was to know about how they played the game. I was free to take notes on any of the lectures held by the individual coaches.

It was a good education and I consider it one of the best breaks I ever had. I had known football before I got the job or obviously I wouldn't have gotten it, but by the time the first Browns training camp was over I think I could have become a coach.

In addition to Paul, one of the great men in football history, there were assistants like Blanton Collier and Weeb Ewbank, who were to become successful head coaches themselves. Many of Brown's players have become out-standing coaches. The most notable in the current era is Don Shula, who has done a remarkable job with the Miami Dolphins.

All you've just read has to do with preparing for the job of broadcasting a football game. Let's go up to the booth now and do a game on *radio*.

The diagram above shows you the position of the crew in the booth. As play-by-play man you will have your spotters and boards on either side of you. You will find it helpful to have a yellow legal pad on which you can jot down the yardage after each play. For example:

Dallas	20	1st and 10
	23	2nd and 7
	31	1st and 10
	30	2nd and 11
	40	3rd and 1
	43	1st and 10

As you can see, the Cowboys have the ball for six plays and are moving on a drive that started on their own twenty. Keep this information in longhand and it will do two things that add to your broadcast. You will automatically give the down and yardage after each play. You will also keep abreast of the drive so you can say, "Dallas drove eighty yards in eleven plays for the touchdown." You can also make note of a spectacular play so you can add: "Thomas sparked the drive with a brilliant thirty-yard run."

In radio coverage remember that *your* descriptive phrases provide the picture for the viewer.

ANNOUNCER: The Cowboys have the ball first and ten on their own twenty-yard line—here they come out of the huddle and up to the line. Staubach crouches back of the center—Thomas and Hill are the setbacks and Alworth is flanked on the right side. Staubach takes the snap and hands off to Thomas driving over right tackle. He finds an opening and drives for short yardage out to the twenty-three-yard line, where Butkus brings him down hard . . . it's a gain of three . . . make it second and seven . . . the Cowboys like to establish their running game early. Alworth comes to the left side this time . . . Staubach flips right to Hill, who swings around right end . . . he shakes a tackler at the line of scrimmage . . . squirms to the outside and carries out to the thirty-one-yard line and its first and ten for the Cowboys.

Vary your delivery. There are any number of ways of describing the way tackles are made, blocks are thrown, passes are caught. Utilize your imagination in finding the best descriptive phrase to fit the occasion. Just as the player works at getting "up" for the game, so should the broadcaster. You are working once a week and describing a game that has constant drama and suspense. Broadcast it that way.

You must always keep your eye on the ball and report its progress. If you look somewhere else you are going to lose the flow and continuity of your description. When an exceptional quarterback fakes well enough so that you have the wrong man with the ball, correct yourself.

Television coverage is a different medium, and I can't stress this enough. There is no need to get into a radio type description. Some announcers will say on a kickoff: "He's at the ten, the twenty, the thirty, etc." It's all right but it isn't really necessary.

When you cover a game on television you can personally see much more of the game than when you cover on radio. This can be important in your comments on coverage. For example, if a quarterback fades to pass, you can immediately look to see which routes the receivers are running and often you know immediately who will get the ball. If it is a draw play, in which the quarterback hands off to a running back, you are not in trouble because you don't have to identify immediately, whereas on radio you would be lost under similar circumstances. The TV announcer must subordinate himself to the picture, which truly tells the story. Name the ball carrier, the tackler, give the down and the yardage, tell who is flanked right or left, but let the picture do much of the talking for you.

In recent years, television networks have done away with using the same announcer for a given team. Formerly a man would do all the games for one team during a season. That has been changed, with mixed emotions on the part of the fans.

Some fans, having become accustomed to the same announcer, miss him. Sometimes a broadcaster who doesn't cover a team regularly doesn't know the personnel, and thus isn't as quick and/or accurate. The counterargument is that by varying announcers you get a more objective report of the game because the man is not emotionally involved with "his" team.

In December 1963 at Chicago's Wrigley Field, I was assigned to cover the first closed circuit telecast of an N.F.L. championship game between the Bears and the Giants. Nate Halpern, president of Theatre Network Television in New York, had set up three Chicago locations where fans who couldn't be at Wrigley Field could watch on closed circuit. Halpern, Commissioner Pete Rozelle, and fifteen thousand others watched the first quarter from McCormick Place. I was working with Bill Osmanski, a onetime great Bears running back, and we were attempting to do the game as we would on any telecast. We had a phone call early in the first quarter that the fans in McCormick Place were responding just as though they were at the field, crowd noise and all. So we quickly adjusted to the situation, which meant that I basically did the job a public-address announcer would do at the field. "Bull carried . . . Modzelewski on the tackle." That was it. Anything else would have been drowned out by the reaction from the auditorium crowd.

A word of caution: Don't ever let personal emotions overrule your sense of judgment and taste in covering a sporting event. Example: I broadcast a game between the Browns and the Packers before eighty-four thousand at

Cleveland Stadium. Fans were getting hotel rooms in Erie, Pennsylvania, Columbus, Ohio, and who knows where else to watch the game. It was crucial and I was the "voice of the Browns." Midway in the fourth quarter the Packers were ahead, 49 to 7. They had played what Vince Lombardi referred to later as a perfect game. They carried out all their assignments exactly as they were put on the blackboard and belted the Browns from goalpost to goalpost. Paul Hornung went out of the game and was replaced by a rookie running back. I was down, dismayed by the performance of the team, and I said, "Here comes Elijah Pitts from Philander Smith . . . and I'm not sure whether that's a college or a guy."

This was crude and tasteless and you can be sure I soon found out about both Philander Smith and Elijah Pitts. The former is an excellent college in Little Rock, Arkansas, and Pitts went on to become a competent running back in the N.F.L.

The comment was not meant as a personal jibe. It was just an outpouring of the way I felt over the way the game had gone, but the remark would have been better left unsaid. In the words of Archie Bunker, it should have been stifled. People don't care how the announcer feels about the outcome. Just do the game.

To sum up, have your own game plan for football. Like the coaches and players, you will be no better than the preparations you've made during the week.

CHAPTER 4

Basketball

The girders in the North Quincy High School gym when I went there were so low that the North players would throw line drives at the hoop from twenty feet out. This is what the sports pages call exploiting the home court advantage.

Henry Hibbard, the senior star when I was a sophomore, was even more sophisticated in his approach. Henry threw the basketball over the girder in a high arc and even when he missed, the crowd loved the shot.

I learned basketball by watching the varsity play and practice in that antiquated gym. This was of great help in later years when I telecast the games of the Akron Goodyears of the Midwest Industrial League and broadcast the Ohio high school championships on a statewide network.

Certain broadcasting fundamentals apply in every sport. In basketball on the professional level, as in football and baseball, press guides, publicity releases, and the usual flood of publications are available. It is essential to familiarize yourself with these tools.

Knowledge of the rules is mandatory. So is an understanding of the game's strategy. The purpose of this text is not to cover these areas. Answers to questions about rules can be found in the rule book. Answers to questions on strategy will come from observing the game.

COACH JIM TURVENE — UNIV OF DAYTON GRAD
CAME TO CHAMINADE IN 1961

WON 25
LOST 1

DAYTON CHAMINADE
EAGLES

BEAT
WARREN 68-60
HARDING

MIKE **BOCKRATH** 22	CO-CAPT AL **BERTKE** 24
SR 6-3 185 14 LAST NITE	SOPH 6-1 180 10 LAST NITE
MIKE **DUFFY** 40	TOM **KEATING** 30
JR 6-1 155	SR 6-1 175
	BARRY **RYDER** 42
	JR 6'1 155

4 MEN IN DOUBLE FIGURES LAST NITE

GARY **ARTHUR** 50 9 PTS LAST NITE (SEASON) LOW
SR 6-5 210
JOE **BALLMAN** 52
JR 6-4 -190

½ OF 12 MAN SQUAD ON HONOR ROLL

CO-CAPT JIM **GOTSCHALL** 20	JERRY **GOTSCHALL** 10
SR 6-2 170 15 LAST NITE	SR 6-2 170
JIM **DIKITO** 12	STEVE **COOK** 14
SR 5-11 165	JR 5-11 165
	JIM **SWEISLER** 32
	SR 5-8 135

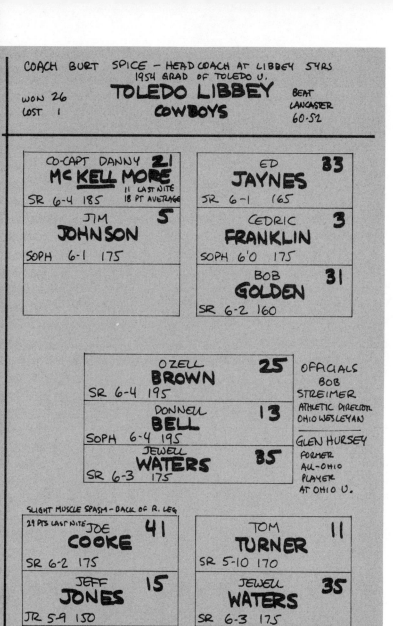

COACH BURT SPICE - HEAD COACH AT LIBBEY 5 YRS
1954 GRAD OF TOLEDO U.

TOLEDO LIBBEY
COWBOYS

WON 26
LOST 1

BEAT
LANCASTER
60·52

CO-CAPT DANNY **21**
MC**KELL MORE**
11 LAST NITE
18 PT AVERAGE
SR 6-4 185

JIM **5**
JOHNSON
SOPH 6-1 175

ED **33**
JAYNES
JR 6-1 165

CEDRIC **3**
FRANKLIN
SOPH 6'0 175

BOB **31**
GOLDEN
SR 6-2 160

OZELL **25**
BROWN
SR 6-4 195

DONNELL **13**
BELL
SOPH 6-4 195

JEWELL **35**
WATERS
SR 6-3 175

OFFICIALS
BOB
STREIMER
ATHLETIC DIRECTOR
OHIO WESLEYAN

GLEN HURSEY
FORMER
ALL-OHIO
PLAYER
AT OHIO U.

SLIGHT MUSCLE SPASM - BACK OF R. LEG
29 PTS LAST NITE JOE **41**
COOKE
SR 6-2 175

JEFF **15**
JONES
JR 5-9 150

LOUIS **23**
ELLIS
JR 5-10 150

TOM **11**
TURNER
SR 5-10 170

JEWELL **35**
WATERS
SR 6-3 175

You can see it all at a glance.

If there is a specific rule that confuses you or strategy that you don't understand, you should ask a player, coach, or official. Too often broadcasters who aren't sure of something hesitate to ask because they are afraid they may appear stupid. I've had confusing situations come up in all sports and have made it a point to seek the answer from the participants while it is fresh in my mind.

I feel that the toughest job in covering basketball is broadcasting a game in which none of the players are familiar to you. For years I covered the semifinals and finals of the Ohio high school basketball championships out of St. John's Arena in Columbus. Some broadcasters would do every game of the tournament live for their local stations, an even tougher assignment.

Because of other commitments, I would arrive in Columbus on the day of the semifinals. This means I'd have to pick things up in a hurry.

In the the theater, an actor who can learn his lines in a fast reading is called a quick study. That's exactly what a basketball announcer has to be in this situation. You have the names and numbers of the players on a small spotting board, but the game moves too quickly to use a spotter. The first time you see the players is when they come out for the pregame warm-up. Most of the time they're wearing jackets, so you can't catch the numbers. Meanwhile, you're getting ready to go on the air and are located smack on the gym floor with thousands of fans screaming in your ears.

The minute the jackets come off you should start working on the numbers. At the same time you try to associate each player with a physical characteristic. Johnny Jones, the tallest player, is blond and has a taped right knee. George Smith, the smallest, has an Afro haircut and is the one who brings the ball up the court most of the time.

If possible, you will have learned this by talking with the coaches during the week. In addition, you will have read the advance stories and seen photos in the papers, and may have identified players in the hotel lobby during the day.

The point is that the basketball announcer, like the player, must scramble and improvise and make quick decisions. If it sounds somewhat frightening and haphazard, you might as well know that it is, but somehow you get the job done.

If you have a color man with you, he can keep track of individual scoring and how many personals a player has. If you are working at one of the smaller stations, it is quite possible that you will not have a color man, so it is essential that you get someone to keep statistics.

Statistics are ultra-important in basketball, particularly in the area of individual fouls. If a player gets into foul trouble early it can have a definite effect on how aggressively he will play thereafter. The coach may have to change his strategy so that one of his star players will still be in there in the late going.

Before the game starts, again assuming that you will be working alone, you will need to line up a guest for half time. Coaches of other teams, college coaches, writers, and former players are good subjects. It helps if the sponsor will spring for a small gift for these guests.

The actual play-by-play on radio calls for a rapid-fire staccato delivery. You'll be able to stay with the action if you describe the plays simply but quickly.

Johnny Most, longtime radio voice of the Boston Celtics, is a master at staying on top of the play. A typical Most description might go like this:

"Havlicek bringing the ball up, tricky dribbles past Cunningham, bounce pass to White to the right of the key. Jo Jo into the corner—*turns, jumps, shoots, scores.*"

With four words, Most has told you what White did after he got the ball.

Other phrases that Most employs to tell the story:

"Stops, pops—bang."

"Around the rim and out." (Or in, if the basket is good.)

"Frazier up for the shot. He's stuffed by Cowens."

"Monroe goes base line."

"White hits on a running one-hander."

"A turnaround jumper—good."

"Hondo fires from downtown."

The score is important. Give it after each basket. Most does this well by saying. "The basket is good, the Celtics lead by six, 109 to 103."

When a player is a particular high scorer it is worth noting periodically how he is doing. You don't have to mention his point total every time he scores, just often enough to keep the listeners posted, because the high scorer's performance, whether good or bad, will usually have a telling effect on the final score. This is especially true in high school ball.

You'll never have to worry about dead air on a radio basketball broadcast. You'll be talking steadily throughout the action and when the game is over you'll know you've done a night's work. Most, after forty-eight minutes of describing a Celtics game, looks as though he's been chasing John Havlicek for a week. His tie is askew, he's covered with perspiration and has a general air of exhaustion about him.

Television is a whole new ball game, as they say. You still need to identify players, but it's right there on the home screen. There is nothing more irritating than a TV broadcaster who overtalks.

The telecaster won't be able to follow the play on his monitor, but he can occasionally glance at it. Often the director will take a close-up of a player after he's scored a basket and is running upcourt. This is a good time to mention how many points the player has scored.

The camera often closes in on a player as he prepares to shoot a foul. If he is an exceptional foul shooter—like Rick Barry or Jack Marin—you can mention it. Conversely, if the man needs a seeing-eye dog to make two in a row—Wilt Chamberlain might fall into this category—mention this too. On the college and pro levels, public relations men will provide printed statistics showing what each player does from the line.

When doing pro basketball, keep an eye on the twenty-four-second clock so you will be aware when a team is running out of shooting time. The twenty-four-second rule—which lifted the pro game out of the dark ages when it was instituted in the mid-fifties—means a team must shoot the ball within that allotted time or lose possession.

Because of the game's speed, basketball broadcasters develop almost what amounts to a patter in their delivery. They are apt to have a set of standard phrases to use regularly. Here is what I mean by patter:

ANNOUNCER: Jones brings the ball up, guarded by Smith, throws into the right corner to Drago. Drago back to Jones. In to Griffith in a high post, over to White on the left side. He drives, lays it up and in. Tech leads, 2 to 0. State coming back, Fitzgerald with the ball, long pass to Cunningham, intercepted by Jones. He slows it up, looking around, guarded closely by Fitzgerald, loops a pass to Griffith in the key. In the right corner to Drago, he jumps, shoots, scores. Tech ahead, 4 to 0.

Note the completeness and yet the brevity of the description. There is no time for long ponderous phrases or dangling participles. When and if play slows up, or during time-outs, you can discuss strategy. Certain moves, of course, you can call as they happen. For example, if a team goes into a full-court press, or a zone, mention it immediately.

Here is the same sequence as it might be described on television:

ANNOUNCER: Jones with the ball—Drago—back to Jones—Griffith—White—2 to 0, Tech. Fitzgerald for Cunningham—intercepted by Jones—Griffith—to Drago. Tech ahead of State, 4 to 0.

The viewer can see the plays; therefore description is unnecessary. As the game moves along, the need for description won't increase, but there will be more room for a discussion of strategy.

Practice techniques in broadcasting basketball are similar to other sports. An investment in a tape recorder is almost mandatory. Turn the sound off on a telecast and do your own play-by-play from the picture. You can cover local high school games with the recorder and tape radio or television broadcasts of professionals.

Make it a point when listening to pros to concentrate on all aspects of the broadcast. The only way you can learn is to listen closely, then select what you think you can adapt to your style. Above all, follow the bouncing ball.

CHAPTER 5

Hockey

They call them the "Gallery Gods" in Boston—an organization that watches the Bruins games from high in the second balcony. I sat up there often as a boy. We'd get out of school and take the subway in to Boston, and when the doors at the Garden opened, we'd race for the first two rows and then wait a couple of hours for the game to start.

But even though I grew up in this hockey-mad area and the game is one of my favorite sports, I've never had the opportunity to broadcast a game. Fred Cusick, who has done the Bruins for both radio and television, is a highly respected, talented broadcaster, and, in fact, was a fine college player. I'm indebted to him for much of the information in this chapter.

As in all play-by-play work, good preparation is half the battle. A prime requisite is knowledge of the players, which in hockey means fifteen to seventeen men on each team.

Goaltenders, of course, are easy to identify. Almost all wear masks, but have other personal characteristics that make them distinguishable—their height, weight, crouching or standup style, their gloved hand.

Gerry Cheevers of the Bruins, for example, has his

57

mask painted with hundreds of stitches, showing where he might have been cut if he weren't protected.

And the goaltender is constant. He is not shifting on and off the ice, like the rest of the players.

Numbers are an obvious way to identify the players, but the action is sometimes so fast that the numbers are obscured. A broadcaster's knowledge of the individuals is therefore very important. He should know the moves each player makes that are peculiar to that player. He should be aware of physical differences—baldness, long hair, mustache, lean, bulky, aggressive, etc.

A broadcaster should know which players are on which lines. If he sees Phil Esposito on the ice, Ken Hodge and Wayne Cashman will be out there with him, unless it is a power play or penalty-killing situation.

He should know which players generally take the ice in such situations. In Boston, Derek Sanderson was known as a great penalty killer, and you knew that if the Bruins were a man short, Sanderson would be getting some ice time—unless he was in the penalty box, which was not unusual.

The players must be identified instantaneously. Charts are fine in football, but in hockey a broadcaster does not have time to look at a chart or a monitor or get the word from a spotter.

But let's look in on a different hockey broadcast, the one you're more apt to be involved in when you start in the business. You work at a station that features live high school sports, and two days before the state hockey tournament the sales manager gets a sponsor for the games. You're his man at the mike.

Your background? Let's assume it includes a great love of hockey—which doesn't make you unique. You had a taste of the sport as a Pee Wee player and as a manager of your high school team. You have a thorough knowledge of the rules and equipment (such as the variables on the curve in a hockey stick). You've watched all levels of play, from eight-year-olds to the pros. You lack broadcast experience, but you're about to get it.

Let's say Melrose is playing Arlington for the title. As high school players wear helmets and are difficult to distinguish by size, a chart *is* necessary. It should show each player's number, his position, his height, weight, and first name, and what year he is in in school.

You should also meet with the coaches for their thoughts and hockey philosophy, as well as for any information they might give on their players. Any bit of trivia might come in handy during the broadcast, although this shouldn't be something you overdo.

Rehearse the names and numbers and individual characteristics. (Do they shoot left or right? Are they good stick handlers, shooters, checkers, etc.?) Get out to see a practice if you can, although at most smaller stations, you might not be able to do this.

Talking to the Arlington coach, for example, you learn that he depends on a flashy, high-scoring line of Bill Harney, Bob Compton, and Tod Harold. Compton will be used on the power play, will kill penalties, and will see a lot of ice time. In a twelve-minute schoolboy period, he might play nine minutes. Unlike Melrose, which has three equal lines and no particular star, Arlington will seldom use the third line.

Arlington likes to pour it on. It is offense-minded, has four defensemen of about equal ability, and an excellent goaltender in Bill Armstrong.

If expected strategy prevails, Melrose will try to check closely the high-powered Harney-Compton-Harold line of Arlington, even to the point of having one player assigned to watch Compton. Melrose will play conservatively, wait for breaks and penalties, and hope goaltender Norm Young can hold his ground.

The point of all this is that there are different styles and you should be able to spot them, analyze them, and report them. The styles can change from game to game, period to period, even with each line shift, and a broadcaster must be alert to the changes.

One of the selling points of hockey is its continuous action. There are no huddles, no throwing the puck around the infield, no walks to the foul lines. If there is a delay for an offside or a penalty, it is as brief as possible. Seconds after a face-off at center ice, the puck can be in the net. This quickness on the ice calls for a corresponding quickness in the broadcasting booth.

Hockey is not a "by accident" game. Even at the lowest level, the playmaking is part of a design to capitalize on opponents' mistakes or lack of ability.

This playmaking—the patterns out on the ice—should be conveyed by the announcer. The broadcast should not be a mere recital of names—a mumbo-jumbo that sounds like somebody reading a telephone book. A description of Melrose on offense should sound something like this:

ANNOUNCER: Fred Renais [try to use first names, but don't make a big deal out of it] carries to center ice, leads Joe Anson with a pass on the right wing. Anson over the Arlington blue line, shoots in the corner to the right of goaltender Bill Armstrong. The puck rebounds out to Art Alcorn, who fires a wrist shot from twenty feet and scores.

Three points in this description:

1. Locate the puck in a defensive zone in relation to the goaltender—it is either to his right or to his left.

2. Give the approximate distance of the shot in feet. A

goal from twenty feet gives the listener a different mental picture of the action than one from, say, fifty feet.

3. Tell what type of shot it was—a wrist shot, a slap shot, or a backhander. Was it deflected, or did it go in cleanly?

When the crowd noise fades from the goal described above, you recap the action, pointing out that Alcorn's quick shot beat Armstrong to his glove side and that Anson made an excellent shift on sophomore defenseman John Harney to set up the play.

My feeling is that it is simpler for a listener if you locate the action in relation to where the announcer sits, with the puck moving to his left or right.

In the old days, when radio broadcasts of sports events were national in scope, listeners might not have been able to form a clear metal picture of where the announcer's booth was, but nowadays almost all broadcasts are regional and the arena is familiar to listeners.

This method has worked for me in football broadcasts, where the action has a similar down-the-field movement.

When the puck changes from one team to another you need more than just names to describe the action. The broadcast becomes tangled if you have Stapleton passing to Martin, then to Orr, who breaks away. Orr either *intercepted* the pass or *stole* it, or *checked* it away from Martin.

Obviously you can't relate every movement of the puck. Sometimes, with close checking at center ice and neither team able to get up any steam, you can sum up the action —or inaction—in general terms.

Hockey, perhaps even more than most other team sports, lends itself to criticism of officials. The very quickness of the game plus the zealousness of the fans leads to controversy over referees' decisions.

These arguments should stay on the ice and not float up to the broadcaster's booth. Criticism of officials is something an announcer should steer clear of. A referee's point of view is different from yours. Because he is on the ice he gets the tempo of the game firsthand. But his head might have been turned when player A high-sticks opponent B. When the referee turns, all he might see is opponent B slashing player A.

He makes his calls on what he sees. So do you. Don't second-guess him. This should apply to the work of officials in every sport.

The only exception that I can think of happened when baseball's Frank Robinson hit a line-drive foul down the right-field line. Proof that it was foul was Robinson's reaction. He took about three steps, then turned back toward home plate. The umpire, however, waved fair ball, so Frank turned around again and wound up with a double.

This was such an obvious situation I felt it had to be reported. But again, as a general rule it is neither proper nor fair to second-guess officials.

The slam-bang nature of hockey provides an additional challenge to an announcer—the description of a fight or, on a rare occasion, a brawl.

There are fights in other sports, of course, and I've broadcast my share. A Red Sox-Yankee bellringer in 1968 in New York comes quickly to mind, a battle in which players ran out of the bullpen to tackle others and Red Sox outfielder Reggie Smith picked up a Yankee pitcher and dropped him not very gently to the turf.

But in hockey, the dropping of gloves and squaring off is much more common. The temptation is to make each fight seem more like a battle for the middleweight championship of the N.H.L. than what it really is—a waltz-me-around-again-Tillie on skates.

There is more violence in the Ballet Russe than in the

average hockey skirmish, and if you don't think so, put on some skates, go out on the ice, and try to maintain the balance necessary to throw a solid punch. You can't get up enough steam to knock down Twiggy.

But once in a while the combatants land some good blows, especially if they fall to the ice and thus regain some leverage.

If you've listened to a description of hockey fisticuffs, it may amaze you that the home player usually seems to get the better of the going. Or maybe it doesn't amaze you, realities being what they are. But try to remember in describing a fight to apply the same basic rule you use in describing regular hockey action—you are a reporter, telling the audience what is actually happening, not what you or they would like to have happen.

As in other sports, less description is needed for a hockey telecast. In some new N.H.L. cities—St. Louis is an example—the games are simulcast, i.e., the same description goes out over radio and television simultaneously. The theory is that you can't give the fans enough information because many of them are still learning the sport.

The slow-motion replay has been the making of hockey on television. The cost of this equipment is high, and it behooves the broadcaster to make sure that the commentary is just as valuable.

It is impossible, while the action is going on, to look at the monitor during a telecast in any sport. You must follow the ball, or in this case the puck. When play stops, then you can pick up what is on the monitor. However, slow-motion replay is perfect to follow on the monitor.

To broadcast hockey well, you must develop a feel for the game. If you've played the game it helps, but this is not necessary to become a broadcaster in any sport.

Practice all you can. Use a tape recorder at local games, or turn down sound on a televised game.

Get so you can pronounce French names without sounding as though you had a mouthful of crepes suzette. If Yvan Cournoyer comes out Wyvan Kornoyer, you're in big trouble.

Hockey is now beginning to reach into Southern cities and is in the middle of vast expansion. Expansion means more broadcasting jobs, and right now there aren't that many available announcers with the experience or hockey knowledge.

The sport has a big future, and that includes the broadcasting booth.

CHAPTER 6

Golf

I don't know whether televised golf tournaments made Arnie Palmer a millionaire or whether Arnold Palmer made TV golf the success it has become. The answer is probably that each was somewhat responsible for the other's well-being. At any rate, there is no denying that golf on television has come a long way in a relatively short time.

My golf broadcasting has been limited in recent seasons because of baseball duties in the summer. But over the years I have worked for Sports Network on the Phoenix Open, the New Orleans Open, the Doral Open, and the Western Open, as well as the P.G.A. tournament.

Announcing a golf tournament is unlike covering any other sport. You aren't doing play-by-play as such. You don't describe Jack Nicklaus walking to the tee, scratching his head, yawning, etc. The actual action in golf is very brief. Most of what you deal in is anticipation, the possibilities, or, as one announcer calls them, the "what ifs."

This means that a golf broadcaster must be exceptionally well briefed—on both the course and the participants —because much of what he says will be background description.

The P.G.A. provides brochures with background material on the golfers, but the announcer must look for more, either through newspaper features or in conversation with the golfers.

Although an announcer may actually be positioned at only one hole of the tournament, he must know the course, and the best way is to walk it the day before the tournament. He should know every blade of grass on the hole he will be covering. I make it a point to walk the hole with a professional golfer, writing down the yardage distances by using markers, such as trees, bushes, or bunkers. I also have the pro point out the hazards on each of the other holes as well, and which club he would be most apt to use from certain positions.

It is important to study the green. This should be done anew every day, because the pin placement is changed daily and the break of a putt is never the same two days in a row. A pro can help tremendously in aiding you to read the green.

A typical network crew covering a major tournament would consist of around eighty-five men. They are supported by a dozen or more cameras, five to seven miles of camera cable, two or three mobile units, at least two special trailers, as many as four or five specially built TV towers, more than five miles of telephone and microphone wire, and sometimes even a raft to float a camera on a water hazard.

With new equipment available and advances in techniques being made all the time—instant replay, slow motion, and split screen—more and more holes will be covered by television. In the 1972 National Open at Pebble Beach, thirteen of the eighteen holes were televised.

However, the general practice is to follow the action on the final five holes. The success of a tournament, from the television standpoint, depends on the camera coverage.

The announcer's role is necessary and important, but secondary.

Producers of sports events generally agree that a golf tournament is one of the toughest events to cover because of the vast area involved.

An announcer assigned to a golf tournament arrives the day before the event starts—usually a Wednesday because most tour events run Thursday through Sunday. Generally the telecast is of the last two days.

The first order of business is a production meeting at which the producer will specify the assignments; that is, which announcers will cover which holes. The man with the least experience is usually assigned the easiest hole. This means a par three, or if there isn't one in the five finishing holes, the chances are he'll work number 14 or 15.

The anchor man will work the eighteenth and most of the time will be assisted by a well-known former golfer. Chris Schenkel and Byron Nelson are an example of such a team. Sometimes, when a big-name star fails to make the cut, he'll be added to the crew for expertise on the last two days. The cut refers to the cutoff point at the end of the second round. Generally the low 50-to-60 golfers qualify for the next rounds while the rest drop out, or are said to fail to make the cut.

Thursday and Friday afternoons the entire crew—director, producer, cameramen, and announcers—will go through dry runs just as if they were on the air. A great amount of coordination is essential, including the cooperation of the host club in providing assistants to keep us aware of the progress of the field.

The producer and director are key men in a golf telecast. They must decide in an instant which picture has the most impact at that particular time for the home viewer.

They can't afford to miss a key shot, so the cameras have to leapfrog and commentators must be quick and responsive to all that is happening out on the course.

The producer, seated in a control truck remote from the fairways, ties the television bundle together. He calls the video shots in an intricate line of communications. His instructions are beamed to the assistant directors, cameramen, sound technicians, and the four or five commentators who are usually deployed around the greens.

The director sits alongside the producer in the truck. He scans the pictures being fed by each of the cameras. At his direction, a technical director pushes a button that puts the picture from the chosen camera on the air. At the same time, the announcer is alerted that his area of coverage is being televised and that his microphone is open.

The actual preparation for telecasting a golf tournament begins long before the first ball is struck. Months in advance, the producer, director, and a technical supervisor visit the site to make a survey. They decide then how many cameras will be needed and where they should be placed, how much mobile equipment will be required, how many telephone lines should be installed, and where the microphones should be positioned to pick up the crowd.

What finally shows up on the home screen for ninety minutes is the product of some seven hundred man-hours of work and preparation.

As an announcer, your part in all of this will be carried out from a tower, usually placed so you can see the action on one green and the tee area of the next hole.

From the tower, you can look at the monitor and see the same picture as the viewer at home sees. You have your list of starting times, so you know who is coming into view, but unless the players are easily recognized by their mannerisms, you may not know who is who in a particular threesome. It is important, therefore, to ascertain in advance which groups will be coming through your coverage and jot down what each player is wearing, so that you can identify him by his white cap, or red shirt, or whatever. This way, you won't mistake Larry Hinson for Johnny Miller or Orville Moody for Miller Barber.

Strangely enough, golf is one sport in which, for an announcer, silence is often golden. The broadcaster will talk normally as the golfers walk up the fairway, filling time with information on how the tournament stands, what the golfers did on this hole yesterday, what most players are using for their second shot against the stiff breeze, and so on.

But when the golfer settles in for his shot, the best advice, to put it bluntly, is to shut up and let the golfer's actions do the talking. Around the green, the broadcaster often has to speak in a subdued tone, even a whisper. Even then, a golfer about to putt can sometimes hear the broadcaster. I've had men bending over a putt look up at the tower and step away from the ball.

Keeping quiet is not so easy as it might seem. There is a tendency to want to contribute something to the telecast and I've found myself chattering away when I shouldn't be.

There should be no feeling or concern on any part of the broadcast team about who is on the air the most. The anchor man will be, which is why he was chosen for the job. And there is nothing more irritating to the viewer than an announcer yakking away while a man is trying to putt. Remember that most people who watch golf tournaments play the game themselves. They don't need your extraneous comments.

Once at the Cleveland Open, I was in a small group watching Jack Nicklaus study a putt. He was on the eighth green, which was close to a refreshment stand. Nicklaus walked around and looked at the putt from all angles in his very deliberate way. Finally he addressed the ball and just as he was about to stroke it, someone at the refreshment stand said, in a normal tone of voice, "Two hot dogs, please."

Under the circumstances, it was like sixty thousand people roaring at Yankee Stadium. Jack backed away from the ball, grinned, and said: "Now we have to go through the whole mess all over again." Whereupon he went through his usual three-minute routine before stepping up and sinking the putt.

Another tendency of some broadcasters is to wax poetic over every shot, which soon dulls the edge of brillance that the golfers actually possess. These men are, after all, professionals, and because they hit an eight iron twenty feet from the pin is not sufficient cause for gasping and flag-waving. If anything, the normal golf shot should be underplayed, or at least should speak for itself, so that when a truly great one comes along, as it will, you can really emphasize it with honesty. Cry wolf too often and the viewer won't believe you when a golfer actually does pull off a fine shot.

In addition to the television network assignments involving the actual golf coverage, there are offshoots of the tournament that call for coverage by local stations. Local announcers, for example, will come out to the course for radio and/or TV interviews.

The local man has his own set of problems in this connection. Touring golfers probably meet more people in the country-club atmosphere than most athletes do in their particular sphere. They travel from city to city, week to week, and the faces of the media are always new. Naturally, the local announcer is going to seek the "big name" player for his interview, but the big name is not always available. If he's had a bad round, he is available but in a bad mood. It often takes diplomacy, luck, and a great deal of tact to come up with a good local interview.

I've always made it a point in interviewing a golfer, even if I've had him on the air three or four times before, to go up to him and say, "Hello, Jack, Ken Coleman, nice to see you again." This takes him off the hook if your face looks familiar but he can't recall the name.

Other local station jobs call for assigning a man to describe the action steadily from the course for a couple of hours, or to have reports broadcast back by an announcer on the eighteenth green, who comes in periodically with scores and interviews.

How to practice broadcasting a golf tournament? The best way, to me, is that old standby—turning the sound down on the telecast and doing the audio yourself, on tape. You could, of course, follow a foursome of friends around a course and announce the action into a tape recorder. This would be good practice and might provide some locker-room laughs if the foursome hits the ball the way most of us do.

To sum up coverage of a golf tournament: Just as the golfer with the least amount of shots is the winner, so, too, is the announcer with the least amount of words.

CHAPTER 7

A Sporting Variety

"The next event I do is the most important event there is."
This has always been my attitude, one I believe is vital
for the growth and success of the young announcer and one
that shouldn't be ignored by the established old pros. You
never know when you'll be called on to announce an un-
familiar sport. You'll have to learn very fast. And you may
even have to refuse an assignment. Whatever the case, I
cover a potpourri of sports in this chapter. Any of them
could one day be your assignment.

BOXING

There was a fairly good crowd on hand that night in the
Providence Auditorium. One of the bouts featured this
promising kid from Brockton, Massachusetts, who was
going to fight Artie Donato, of Red Bank, New Jersey.
Next to me at ringside was a man who was going to start
broadcasting the fights the following week. He had brought
along a tape recorder to practice, but didn't get much of
an opportunity.

The kid from Brockton was Rocky Marciano, and about a minute after the opening bell, Donato was on the deck, his mouthpiece was on its way out of the ring, and the fight was over. Donato, as many others were to be in the future, had been the victim of Rocky's left hook.

Boxing is tough to do on radio, one of the toughest. It is simply a fact that no matter how fast you can talk, fighters throw punches faster. Boxing is the only sport I know where the announcer can't keep up with the action.

However, Don Dunphy stayed with it better than anyone else. Dunphy did many of the big fights. I sat next to him the night Carmen Basilio beat Johnny Saxton in Cleveland, and Dunphy was outstanding.

I'll also never forget Basilio that night. Two days before, I had interviewed him for NBC's *Monitor* when he was working out at a gym in Cleveland. He came across then as a pleasant, almost placid man. But against Saxton he was something completely different. I've seen psyched-up football players, but Basilio was more than psyched up. He was like a caged lion and fought that way.

Dunphy was excellent, but as I said, on a radio broadcast of a bout, you simply can't tell it all. Don had a rapid-fire delivery and a special gimmick—a concoction of honey that he'd take between rounds so his voice wouldn't give out.

Television requires a thorough knowledge of the background of the fighters and an ability to relate what is happening now as compared with what happened a year ago or five years ago.

Analysis is also important. Was the fighter hurt by the right cross or did the punch look better than it was? Has the fighter come back from adversity before? Who likes to take the lead? And so on. The staccato style of the radio broadcast is not needed. What is needed is a calmness, an analytical approach that will make sense out of the battle in front of the viewer.

HORSE RACING

I asked veteran broadcaster Jack Drees one day which sport he thought was the toughest to cover. I expected him to say boxing, but he fooled me. The toughest, said Drees, was horse racing. He's done the Kentucky Derby a number of times and as he put it, "There you are. It all happens in a couple of minutes, millions of people are watching, and you had better be right."

To be right you have to memorize the colors of the jockeys' silks, not an easy task. The good public-address system announcers at the tracks must memorize these colors for at least eight different races each day. I suppose it becomes routine, but when I worked the Marshfield and Weymouth Fairs, I tried the memory lane, and it was tough going.

Most announcers have binoculars on the horses as soon as they come out on the track, and keep repeating aloud each horse's name and its colors.

There have been many great racing broadcasters. Certainly one of the best was Fred Capossela. In the book *Voices of Sport*, by Maury Allen, reference is made to Fred's fantastic memory.

"Five minutes after the race is over," says Capossela, "I don't have the slightest idea who ran in it or who won." As soon as the race ends, he wipes it and the colors out of his mind and starts to work on the next race.

Capossela broke in with the late Bryan Field and has been involved in all the big races. He has said that he never bet on a race in his life, certainly an excellent way to remain objective.

BOWLING

One morning, while still working in Cleveland, I had a call from Marvin Sugarman in New York. Sugarman, a respected television producer, wanted to know if I would be interested in a series of bowling shows on a regional network.

I was not really fired up by the idea. I had a busy schedule doing the Indians and Browns, plus daily radio and television shows. Not only that, I knew little or nothing about bowling. My wife finally convinced me that I should take the job to broaden my sphere of sports broadcasting, so I accepted.

I told Sugarman I would give it a try but that I would need a lot of help. Soon afterward, there arrived in Cleveland a man named Ray Hamaleskie, who gave me a crash course in bowling. We went to the local lanes and he taught me the ropes: How to score, difficult situations for the bowler, the terminology of the sport.

He was similar to a spotter in football, and I relied heavily on his knowledge. It turned out to be a successful series, one I enjoyed doing. I also discovered there was a vast and growing TV audence in bowling.

With Ray's help, I was able to describe the event accurately. The bowling commentator is primarily a host. He interviews the bowlers before and after the match and tries to put them at ease.

I might add that it is somewhat embarrassing to be caught putting on makeup in the men's room of a bowling alley. But that's show biz.

SWIMMING AND DIVING

Dick Bailey, who put together what is now the Hughes Sports Network, asked me one day to go to New Haven to work on the N.C.A.A. swimming and diving championships. Even though one of my hobbies is snorkeling and I have spent hours under the sea, I had never broadcast anything remotely resembling a swim meet, with the possible exception of a Browns-Giants game one rainy afternoon in the Polo Grounds.

As was the case with Marv Sugarman on bowling, I felt an obligation to tell Dick I didn't have any experience in this area. That seemed no problem to him. He told me I'd get all the help I needed and he was right.

The producer and director of the telecast were Joe O'Rourke and Joe Samel, two men I'd worked with on football and golf. The "expert" on the show was Bob Rambo. Bob, a member of the Olympic swimming committee for the 1964 games and an instructor in physical education at the University of Pennsylvania, was also the diving coach at Penn.

Our job at New Haven was not an easy one. We were to videotape with commentary all the events over a three-night period. At the end of competition, about eleven o'clock Saturday night, all this material would be cut down to run as an hour show on a network of stations the next day. For the technical people it was a case of working under the gun. For me it was a matter of cramming everything I could into my head, by talking with Rambo and by reading about the competitors and talking to them.

With Rambo's expertise, especially in the diving competition, everything worked out fine.

TENNIS

The sport of tennis has been around for a long while, but only recently has broadcasting been a factor in it. Television and tennis go well together, and from Wimbledon, Forest Hills, Longwood, and other tennis centers, the game has been beamed into the living room.

Bud Collins, columnist and tennis expert for the Boston *Globe*, is the dominant name in tennis telecasting and does an outstanding job. Collins, virtually a walking encyclopedia on tennis matters, nevertheless rereads the rules every year, because knowing them is of utmost importance in broadcasting a match.

"You're up there in the booth with egg on your face if a controversy arises and you're hazy on a rule," he says.

Other Collins by-laws:
• Don't talk too much.
• Call them as you see them. If you think an official erred, say so, politely.
• Know your players—their past performance, their strong and weak points, their personalities.
• Be a reporter, not a gusher and a Pollyanna.
• Don't show up your broadcasting partner by referring to mistakes he might have made.
• Admit it when you've made a mistake.

MAKING A FILM

Another type of work that is not necessarily connected with broadcasting but will quite likely get you on the air involves the making of a promotion film.

Today this work is expertly handled for pro football by NFL Films Inc. I used to put together a film of Browns highlights each year in Cleveland with John Borza, the superientendent of audiovisual education for the Cleveland public schools. It took about six weeks of steady work, poring over films, to put together forty minutes of excitement that could be shown to groups or over television. John would edit the film, Harold Sauerbrei, the public-relations man, would write the script, and, quite frankly, it would be done with the idea of making the Browns look as good as possible. It was, after all, *their* promotional movie. Putting the sound to the film took hours of rehearsal and about a day's work when we went to the film studio in Chicago.

CUTTING A RECORD

After the 1967 season, when the Red Sox won the American League pennant, I was involved in the making of a record called *The Impossible Dream*. Written by the late John Connelly and produced by Carlo Lagrotteria of our radio staff, the record sold by the thousands, particularly in the New England area.

When Harvard and Yale played their 29 to 29 tie in 1968—a game voted one of the ten most exciting college games of all time—we made another recording, featuring excerpts from the play-by-play broadcast, which I had done.

We have covered a number of different sports and by-products in this chapter, and there are more. The main point I am making is that there will be times you will be called upon to do a job in a field in which you are not an expert. A pro will accept the challenge. If you become known as a broadcaster who can handle any kind of work, your market value increases and so does your reputation.

Sports announcers in smaller areas usually do all kinds of programs—news, record shows, man-on-the-street interviews. It is a great training ground.

After stating the above, however, let me say it is not a bad idea to file the following thought for future reference: If you become successful in broadcasting and start working on the major league level, it is possible to spread yourself too thin. You can take on more work than you can handle.

It is also possible that there will be some sports that you

will discover are simply not your bag. You could wind up looking bad by taking on the assignment. Don't be like the girl in *Oklahoma* who "just cain't say no." Sometimes no is the wisest answer.

CHAPTER 8

The Daily and Weekly
Sports Show

Famous newscaster Lowell Thomas, when asked how long
it took him to prepare his daily program, replied: "You
might say twenty minutes, or you might say twenty years."

Thomas couldn't have put it better. You don't measure
a broadcaster's work in time spent. Today's broadcast depends in large part on last week's experience and the
thoughts you might have had while driving home yesterday.
In other words, the job is with you, sometimes subconsciously, most of your waking hours.

For my radio show, I arrive at the studio a couple of
hours before air time. However, if I'm going to use what we
call a "think" piece or a commentary, I'll try to write
a good part of it at home. It's quiet there, and concentration comes easier. A newsroom in a radio station can be a
hectic place.

When I get to the station, I'll clear the wire—that is,
go through the material sent over the Associated Press and
United Press International teletypes—putting aside stories
interesting enough to use on the broadcast.

I'll then rewrite the hard news in my own style. Hard
news? That's the immediate news—the scores, trades, big
games coming up that night, deaths of prominent athletes,

injury reports. In other words, any sports happening vital enough to warrant being given to the listener immediately.

One of the temptations in using wire copy is to "rip and read," meaning to read the stuff over the air without rewriting.

If an announcer says he's never done this, he's probably bending the truth, because there are occasions when the ideas just won't come. That's when the wire service becomes your crutch, your security blanket.

Other times, a late-breaking story simply leaves no time for rewriting. A good example is a Saturday night in October, with football scores and stories pouring in. In such a case, it's better to get the facts over the air rather than try to be fancy.

Selectivity is the key word in a radio show, because most sportscasters don't have a great amount of air time. Fifteen minutes is a luxury, and most broadcasts are limited to five or ten.

Therefore, what you leave out of a broadcast is, in a sense, as important as what you put in. Experience and a feel for what you think listeners will be interested in are your only guidelines.

In Boston I have had two daily radio shows—a five-minute program at 5:05 P.M., and a ten-minute one at 6:15. Both are basically sports news shows, not commentary, in which I deal with what has happened or will be happening that day.

Some broadcasters thrive on controversy, and go heavy on the commentary during their show. Controversy, of course, is a quick and easy way to gain attention. The danger is that it can become manufactured sensationalism, created conflict. If a broadcaster is accurate in his comments, fine, but I personally don't seek out controversy. If it is news I'll report it, but I won't belabor the subject.

In Boston, for example, controversy often revolves

KEN DOLEMAN SHOW FORMAT

TUESDAY'S

6:30 - 6:45 PM

TO: WTAM AND SPECIAL NET ----- RECORD FOR DB STATIONS

ORIGIN: _____

- -

LOCAL BILLBOARD:

MUSIC: BE A BOOSTER UP 11 SEC AND CLIP FOR:

WTAM ANNCR: WTAM presents the Ken Coleman Show----in his ex-
               clusive interviews with your Cleveland Brown's
               team members----brought to you by the friendly
               Stewart Warner Radio and TV Dealer in your
               neighborhood.

BUSINESS: NETWORK STATIONS JOIN HERE AT APPROX 6:30:18 FOR:

NETWORK BILLBOARD:

MUSIC: BE A BOOSTER UP 15 SEC AND FADE B.G. FOR

COLEMAN: Hello Fans. This is Ken Coleman all set to chat
               with the champions. We're going to be talking
               with members of the Cleveland Browns Football
               Team as we bring you special transcribed inter-
               vews from the locker room of the Cleveland Browns
               at League Park in Cleveland, Ohio. We'll have
               our first interview in just a moment.

BUSINESS: NETWORK STATIONS CUTAWAY HERE AT APPROX. 6:30:45

               FOR: LOCAL COMMERCIAL (TIME: 1:00)
                           TWO BEAT PAUSE: THEN:

BUSINESS: NETWORK STATIONS REJOIN AT APPROX. 6:31:45

               AFTER WORD CUE:

A typical format for the daily show.

"And you can own Stewart Warner TV for as little
as _____ including tax and full guarantee."
(TWO BEAT PAUSE)

COLEMAN: FOOTBALL INTERVIEWS FOR APPROX 5:00 MINUTES

BUSINESS: NETWORK STATIONS CUT AWAY AT APPROX 6:37 ON
             WORD CUE:

                     "But first here is a word of importance
             to you."

COLEMAN: STEWART WARNER 1:15 MINUTE COMMERCIAL
             TWO BEAT PAUSE: THEN:

BUSINESS: STAIONS REJOIN AT APPROX. 6:38:15 AFTER WORD CUE.
                     "So hurry to your Stewart Warner Dealer
             for your entry blank and all the rules of the
             Stewart Warner Football Contest."

COLEMAN: COLEMAN INTERVIEW APPROX 5:00 MINUTES

BUSINESS: NETWORK STATIONS CUT AWAY AT APPROX 6:43:15 ON
             WORD CUE:

                     "Thank you _____ for being with
             us."

COLEMAN: READ FINAL STEWART WARNER COMMERCIAL -- 50 SEC.

MUSIC:_ _ _ _BE A BOOSTER INSTRUMENTAL_ UP_THEN FADE_FOR_ _ _

WTAM ANNCR: The Ken Coleman Show was brought to you by the
             friendly Stewart Warner TV Dealer in your neighbor-
             hood. Join us again next week at this time when
             Ken Coleman -- chats with the champions.

MUSIC:_ _ _ _BE A BOOSTER _UP TO CLOSE_ _

around how athletes—particularly the Red Sox—get along with one another. Reams of copy and hours of air time have been devoted to the subject, but I feel this aspect of pro sports is vastly overrated. Some of the unhappiest teams were also the greatest.

An example was the Yankees under Casey Stengel. Stengel, with a wagonload of talent, liked to platoon. He thought the idea was terrific—indeed, he won pennants with it—but his players were of another mind. Each one naturally wanted to play every day. However, they were pros and, when they were in the lineup, played like pros. Because the talent was there they won championships.

This is not to say that a well-thought-out commentary on a controversial subject is not good sports show fare. But don't overdo a good thing. Have steak every day and it becomes commonplace.

I've found that an occasional phone interview can pick up the daily radio sports show. After the 1971 World Series, I talked with Pirates pitching hero Steve Blass, who is from Connecticut. When Paul Harney from the Pleasant Valley Country Club near Worcester, Massachusetts, won the San Diego Open, I talked with him. As "locals," they had special appeal to my New England listeners.

Sometimes an interview with someone close to a sports hero works out even better. In Cleveland, I phoned Bill Mazeroski's mother in Barberton, Ohio, the day Bill hit the home run that gave the Pirates the world championship in 1960.

Because I travel so much with the Red Sox, my radio shows often have to be done from out of town, by telephone. Here, my association with the players comes in handy. I see them around the hotel during the day and it becomes a simple matter to be up to date on injuries, batting slumps, managerial problems, and the general well-being of the team. When I call in my show, I can check with the newsroom for late-breaking stories in other sports.

Some sportscasters use professional writers to help them prepare material. There is certainly nothing wrong with this, but I feel more comfortable writing my own scripts and delivering my own words.

Often I'll write material I won't use right away—a feature or an offbeat story. When an idea hits, it's wise to get it down on paper and set the story aside for one of those dry days when the mind draws a blank.

One of the never-ending arguments about a play-by-play broadcaster who also has a daily sports show is his allegiance to the team he travels with. Am I, for example, inhibited in my remarks regarding the Red Sox because I'm a play-by-play announcer for them?

On those play-by-play broadcasts, my job, as I've said before, is to report the action. However, on my shows I have the right to venture opinions and comment on performance.

Before the 1972 season, in a series on the Red Sox, I discussed their strengths and weaknesses. I questioned, for instance, whether thirty-eight-year-old Luis Aparicio had enough range to cover shortstop the way he once did, and whether the Red Sox had given up too much hitting talent in a big midwinter trade with Milwaukee.

The Red Sox front office has never told me what to say or not to say on a daily sports show. I feel that worrying about pressure from above is a hangup that leads nowhere. I've been at this business too long to get caught in the security merry-go-round. Security is an inner feeling that comes from accepting yourself as a professional in sports announcing or any other business.

You know if you're doing a good job.

Getting back to the daily sports show, television has one big advantage over radio—the use of visual material. Films and videotapes of game action are invaluable and should be used as much as possible. A television show which merely features the broadcaster's face for ten minutes is not doing justice to the medium. Such a show might as well be on radio.

You've often seen television sports programs in which scores are shown in a manner similar to a restaurant menu. Meanwhile, the announcer is repeating the scores. Here again, the show is not using television to its fullest. The least the broadcaster can do in such an instance is give a sentence or two of amplification as each score rolls past on the screen—who got the big hit, who had the homers, who was the winning pitcher.

A TV sports show must also use more interviews. If the Knicks beat the Celtics in a playoff game, the enterprising broadcaster will be in the locker room interviewing one of the principals. Immediacy is important, but even eight or ten hours later, such an interview is of great value on a television show.

And one final note on TV broadcasters. The old movie cliche of the announcer with his hat tilted on the back of his head, tie askew, and a cigarette dangling from his lips just won't work nowadays. A man's personal appearance and grooming are important, even to the use of make-up when doing a studio show.

A relatively new type of daily program, usually done on radio, but once in a while on TV, is the talk show. Listeners call in and talk informally with the program host. Most callers have strong opinions on sports subjects and are anxious to engage the host in what is politely called debate.

In Boston, where sports fans are quite knowledgeable, hockey is a big favorite, and its devotees most emotional. Talk show callers are vociferous in their opinions concerning the Bruins.

Talk show hosts have a tough job. They are expected to be a fount of information ("What color trunks did

Sonny Liston wear in the Lewiston, Maine, fight?") and right on top of current sports news. At the same time, they must be smooth enough to cut off the long-winded caller and must be able to deal with criticism of their own ideas without flying off the handle.

Some hosts have strong opinions, while others allow the caller to express his views without commenting on them. Some even have been known to say, "I don't know," in answer to a tough question.

A background as a writer, reporter, and interviewer is fundamental to anyone who aspires to be a talk show host. Incidentally, the field is so narrow that it would be unwise to zero in on such a career without being in the broadcasting business first. Then, if the opportunity knocks, you are there.

Guy Mainella, who runs one of the most successful talk shows in Boston, points out that a host must develop a good conversational approach. He must listen to what other people are saying and not think out his own position while the caller is talking.

Mainella feels that the most important part of a talk show is to treat people decently. Some of the questions might be silly, but some of the answers won't be so clever either.

The role of a host is to lead a sports discussion, not to dominate it. Controversy is the heart of the program, but don't force it. It will come naturally, simply because if you are doing your job you may express opinions that run counter to those generally held.

Talk shows are usually done on a twelve-second delay. Everything is recorded on two tape machines and delayed twelve seconds before it goes on the air in order to filter obscenity, libel, or slander. The last two are the serious problems, because it is a simpler matter to recognize the obscenity.

PAUL BROWN SHOW
THURSDAY'S

6:30-6:45 PM
OCTOBER 2, 1952
TO: WTAM AND SPEC NET ---- RECORD FOR PLAYBACK STATIONS

- -

LOCAL BILLBOARD:
MUSIC:_MR._TOUCHDOWN_USA_ UP_11 SEC AND CLIP_FOR:

COLEMAN: The Paul Brown Show .... brought to you by
            the Warner and Swasey Company one of the
            world's largest manufacturers of machine tools.

BUSINESS: NETWORK STATIONS JOIN HERE AT APPROX 6:30:18 FOR:
NETWORK BILLBOARD:
MUSIC:_MR._TOUCHDOWN_USA_ THEME UP_15 SECS_AND_FADE B.G. FOR

COLEMAN: Hello, fans. This is Ken Coleman. We're all
            ready to bring you a little football discussion
            with the man who can really give us an insight
            into what makes a football team click ... Paul
            Brown, head coach and general manager of the
            Cleveland Browns!
BUSINESS: NETWORK STATIONS CUTAWAY HERE AT APPROX 6:30:45
          FOR: LOCAL COMMERCIAL (TIME: 45 SECS)
                 TWO BEAT PAUSE; THEN:

 COLEMAN: WARNER AND SWASEY COMMERCIAL :45 SECONDS
            TWO BEAT PAUSE: THEN:
BUSINESS: NETWORK STATIONS REJOIN AT APPROX 6:31:35 ON
          WORD CUE: I'd suggest you make it a point to
           stop in at Warner & Swasey tomorrow.

The format for the weekly show.

BROWN: (TALKS FOOTBALL FOR 9 MINUTES)

BUSINESS: NETWORK STATIONS CUTAWAY AT APPROX 6:40:35 ON
          WORD CUE:

          "I'll be back with a final word in a moment."
          TWO BEAT PAUSE: THEN:
COLEMAN: WARNER AND SWASEY 1 MINUTE COMMERCIAL
          TWO BEAT PAUSE: THEN:
BUSINESS: NETWORK STATIONS REJOIN AT APPROX 6:41:39 ON
          WORD CUE: It's conveniently located on East
          55th Street at Prospect. So stop in there
          soon and get all the facts. I suggest you do
          it tomorrow.

BROWN: GIVES APPROX 1 MIN 45 SECS OF PREDICTIONS
BUSINESS: NETWORK STATIONS CUTAWAY AT APPROX 6:43:15 ON
          WORD CUE:
          "Until next week, so long."
          TWO BEAT PAUSE: THEN:
MUSIC:_ _ MR. TOUCHDOWN INSTRUMENTAL_UP & FADE_FOR:

COLEMAN: WARNER AND SWASEY COMMERCIAL (CLOSING) - 25 SECS.

MUSIC:_ _ MR. TOUCHDOWN USA INTRUMENTAL THEME UP BRIEFLY
          THEN_FADE FOR:_

COLEMAN: Now this is Ken Coleman speaking for Paul Brown
          inviting you to join us at this same time
          next week when Warner and Swasey again
          presents .... the Paul Brown Show. Until
          then, so long!

MUSIC:_ _ MR. TOUCHDOWN UP_TO CLOSE

Two phone lines (in a small market) is a minimum, but on the bigger stations, four or five are used, plus an unlisted number for outside calls to athletes or others for interviews.

Talk shows vary in length from fifteen minutes to four hours, but the average one is a couple of hours. That's a lot of talking about sports.

Humor is important in a talk show. The host shouldn't treat sports with the deadly seriousness of a program on drug addiction. Mainella kids around with "rasslin' " and roller derbies and crybaby athletes and topics he feels lend themselves to humor or satire. A pompous broadcaster is just as bad as a pompous anything else—probably worse.

There are also weekly sports shows, both on radio and television. In Cleveland, I was involved in a program called *The Quarterback Club*, a half-hour weekly show that featured filmed highlights of the Browns' games.

Putting such a program together was hard work. After the game on Sunday, I would select from a play-by-play sheet the action to be used in the show. This meant about eighteen minutes of film.

On Monday, the film editor and I would review the game just to make sure we didn't miss something that wasn't on the play-by-play sheet.

After the final decision, the editor would cut the film and I'd write an accompanying script. In the early years we'd do the commentary live, but later we recorded the audio to fit the film.

I'd also have a guest on the program, usually a player who had starred in the game. He would make comments on the action and was especially appreciated during those rare programs when the film broke.

Art Modell, president of the Cleveland Browns, grew up in television as a producer and director before he became a football executive. He had a feel for the medium and was extremely helpful in suggesting ways to improve the show.

Another studio program I did in Cleveland was with Jimmy Brown, the great runner. We had a taped Saturday-night television show, in which Jim had some prepared questions for me to ask him.

Sometimes I'd make suggestions on topics we might discuss. Brown said that when he was new to television the relentless red eye of the camera was a tougher foe than the front four of the Los Angeles Rams. However, he never appeared to be nervous and has evidently become accustomed to cameras in Hollywood.

One of Jim's most interesting shows contained a principle that young announcers could use. Brown pointed out that he studied films of other running backs to pick up helpful ideas.

That works in broadcasting too. Listen to other announcers. Pick up what you think are the good points and discard the bad ones. You will still be your own man and have your own style, plus the best of the rest.

A daily sports show, like anything else, improves with practice. Here are some fundamentals:

- Write your own material.
- Learn to type.
- Time your shows so you can do, say, four minutes and thirty seconds on the button.
- Read aloud as much as possible—everything from poetry to the Yellow Pages. Sometimes the local station will provide copy.

Any good broadcaster will give himself time to rehearse. Before you go on the air, check your copy in the studio. Read it aloud. Sometimes you can catch a mistake in typing so that you don't come across it cold on the air and stumble. You must be completely familiar with the material.

Everyone knows about broadcasting fluffs, the "Hoobert Heevers" and "Sir Stifford Crapps" of the industry. The better ones have been put into best-selling albums.

No broadcaster is immune to these fluffs. You may mispronounce a name or lose your place in a script. Worry in advance about fluffs and you're dead. Often, young announcers are so fluff-conscious they read words instead of expressing ideas.

If you make a mistake, don't get rattled. We all do it. Once on television I was reeling off some golf scores and announced the leader as Dr. Mary Ciddlecoff, instead of Dr. Cary Middlecoff. It broke me up and no doubt left a few viewers weak around the ears.

Unless you're an exception, you'll be nervous when you first get on the air. This is perfectly normal, and over the years you'll always have this feeling, although as you mature the nervousness will bother you less.

So will the fluffs, as sure as my name is Cole Kenman.

CHAPTER **9**

The Art of Interviewing

The Red Sox were playing the Yankees, and as I drove to Fenway Park I was thinking about Mickey Mantle. This was probably going to be the last time he would appear in Boston as a player, and I was anxious to have him on my fifteen-minute radio dugout show before the game. Mantle was not an easy man to get on an interview program. Sometimes before games he had very little to say to the men of the media. Perhaps he was thinking about the game. Maybe he was hurt. Whatever his reasons, he was not usually receptive to interviews.

When I arrived at the ball park, I went to the Yankee dugout and talked with a couple of the players. Then I walked into the clubhouse and Jim Hegan, the Yankee bullpen coach, told me Mantle was in the trainer's room. I went in and said, "Mickey, you've said yourself that this might be your last game in Boston. I'd like to do a show with you." He asked, "When?" I said, "Right now." He said, "How long?" I said, "Oh, not too long." He said okay. We started.

I had seen Mickey Mantle play a lot of baseball and I had read a great deal about his career. The night before he had come to the plate as a pinch-hitter and had received a standing ovation from the crowd at Fenway Park. Like all great players, he had also often been booed. But fans around the country were aware that they would probably not see him again as a player, and he was getting warm receptions in every park.

We talked about that and about many other things. Most athletes are easy to interview, but some are not. It is a matter of their individual personalities. Some of them are just naturally more outgoing than others. Some can be very funny and talkative until they have a microphone in front of them. Then they withdraw. The secret is to know your man, if not personally, then at least by having read about him to know what his interests are and what he likes to talk about. Get him going on what is familiar, easy ground for him and you have the makings of a good interview.

While it is not always possible to do so, whenever you can it is important to plan an interview. You may wonder why this is not always possible. Sometimes you go into a ball park with a specific player in mind, whom you want to interview that day. Maybe he is at a team meeting, or for some other reason is unavailable. Maybe some Hall of Famer happens to be visiting the park and you know it's your only chance all season to get him. You change your plans, and wing it.

When you do have the ideal situation—that is, a player you've planned on—you can do some research before the interview. Even if it happens to be someone you have known for some time, there is something you can usually find out that will make for an interesting discussion.

You may wind up doing interviews anywhere, from the bullpen to the dugout to a manager's office to a whirlpool bath. When I first started doing TV interviews in a studio, which is an ideal controlled situation, I used to write questions on a blackboard off camera, behind the guest. The viewer at home would not see this and it would seem as though I was looking directly at the guest. Most of the time I would be, but when necessary I could take a quick glance at the board if I needed to. The board was simply a crutch, to help with what is the most important part of any interview, namely, to *listen* to what the man has to say when he answers your question.

This brings me to a common and really quite normal fault of the young inexperienced interviewer. He may be nervous, and after he asks a question—while the guest is answering—he is trying to think of his next question. With that blackboard I didn't need to formulate questions in my mind. I was able to listen and as a result go off in different directions if the answers prompted other areas of thought. Then I could get back on the track.

Speaking of going off in different directions, I'm reminded of an interview I did with Casey Stengel one day in Cleveland. This was for a radio show and there was no particular time limit. After Casey had held court with reporters, I caught him alone, a rarity in itself. I asked him for an interview and he said, "Okay, kid, but not too long." I turned on the recorder and posed this question: "Casey, Herb Score is pitching for the Indians today and you are a manager who likes to platoon. How did you decide on your lineup for today's game?"

Casey answered my question by saying that Score was a left-hander and of course Carl Hubbell was a lefty and he pitched over in the National League, and he then proceeded to analyze the National League race. He took twelve minutes to answer the one question, going off on all sorts of tangents, but amazingly he wound up in the last minute or so by getting back to the original question and answering it very well. My only regret was that I didn't save the tape. It was a beauty.

An important aspect of interviewing is to put your guest at ease. Even though a fellow may be an athlete who has performed before thousands, he is not necessarily at home in front of a microphone. This is especially so with a rookie player, who may never have been on the air before. Sometimes you interview outstanding high school athletes and they may be quite nervous. The best way to put your guest at ease is to be at ease yourself. This comes with experience, but it also comes for the young interviewer with proper preparation and the knowledge that he must control the show.

There is a matter of attitude involved in broadcasting just as there is in participating in sports. It can be put many ways, I suppose, but it boils down to having confidence in yourself and believing in your ability. When I was about fifteen years old I was pitching in the Quincy Park League and my older brother Bill gave me some advice that I've never forgotten. He said, "When you go out there on that mound you think to yourself, *I'm the boss here and this ball game belongs to me.*" As many ballplayers who faced me in that league could tell you, I wasn't a very good pitcher. But they had to beat me. I wasn't going to beat myself.

I have taken that attitude, in a much more subtle way, of course, into my broadcasting life and it helps.

There is a big difference between doing interviews on radio and on TV because of the visual possibilities on television.

Fred Glover has had a long career as a player and coach in professional hockey. He once was player-coach of the Cleveland Barons, of the American Hockey League. I used to interview him each year and because I could skate well we provided the viewers with a unique show.

I would arrive at the Cleveland Arena and put on a Barons uniform, and Fred and I would go on the ice. We would start at one end with the cameras rolling and come down the ice, passing the puck back and forth till one of us would fire it into the net. We would both wind up in a swirl of ice right at the goal mouth and I would start the interview.

This accomplished two things. It was an attention grabber that helped my image because it showed I could skate. It also put Glover at ease because he was right there in familiar surroundings and was loose and free.

I try to employ visual techniques whenever I can on TV. I have had Lou Groza show how he had the ball placed and what his stance was when he kicked a football. Jim Brown has demonstrated how he held a football. Once I did an interview with Carl Yastrzemski in a studio while we were playing catch.

Bobby Leo was a great running back at Harvard. I interviewed him one day in a studio while we shot a game of pool. Since pool happens to be one of my hobbies, and Bobby was pretty good at it, this added something to what we were doing.

Ted Williams has gone into hitting techniques on camera and Hoyt Wilhelm has shown how he holds his knuckleball (he actually uses his fingertips). All of these visual aids are helpful for several reasons. Perhaps the main one is that you and your guest get absorbed and interested in what you are talking about and as a result this appeals to the listener or viewer.

Some players are just naturally easy to interview, being cooperative and articulate. Interviewing Brooks Robinson or Harmon Killebrew is like taking the day off. It is no coincidence that they both have interview shows of their own and therefore know the problems the interviewer faces. Ted Williams is one of my favorites. He is a very intelligent man on a number of subjects and he is outspoken.

Vida Blue made an interesting comment during the 1971 season. He said, "I won some ball games and people started asking me questions about everything from politics to war." He brings out a good point. Basically you should talk with a baseball player or any athlete about the sport in which he participates. However, there are times when you may know that a man is familiar with other subjects and you can get involved in asking him questions in these areas. Rick Reichardt, of the White Sox, is an extremely intelligent man. So is Mike Epstein, who was on the champion Oakland A's. Knowing this, I have thrown them questions on such matters as the implications of baseball and other sports as applied to our society. These are questions I wouldn't ask some ballplayers.

Rico Petrocelli set an American League record a couple of years ago for the most home runs by a shortstop, forty. One of the reasons he did it was because of his quick wrists. How did he get those quick wrists? One way was by playing the drums. Rico is a good drummer and a fan of Buddy Rich. So we often discuss music in an interview.

Who would have more knowledge than anyone regarding the speed of players on his team and the respective abilities of the throwing arms of opposing outfielders? The third base coach. He makes a living out of knowing about these things and making the right decision most of the time, so he's a good one to interview for his inside opinion.

Very often I will ask a player if there is a particular question he would like me to ask him so that he can cover a topic he would like to speak out on. I will try to probe around to find if there is something that might be interesting. Sometimes if another player on the team has come up with an outstanding performance I will discuss it with my guest. Often players provide excellent information on other players.

Once, years ago when I was with WNEB in Worcester, Massachusetts, I had Bob Cousy and Easy Ed Macauley on a program together. Macauley is now a sports announcer in St. Louis, and at the time I was aware of the fact that he

was going into broadcasting. So I simply had Ed interview
Cousy and I just sat back and listened.

Whenever I am going to interview someone who may be
involved in a controversial situation, obviously I am going
to ask him about it. I believe in letting him know this
before we go on the air so that he can prepare his answer. Sometimes men in this position are happy to be
interviewed because they can't be misquoted and state-
ments can't be taken out of context.

During the 1971 season Rico Petrocelli got involved
in a conversation with a newspaperman who was a good
friend of his. Rico had a few gripes and he mentioned
them, not knowing that what he was saying was going
to be printed. But it was and made it appear that Petrocelli
was extremely unhappy about a lot of things. He was happy
to go on the air and straighten them out. In fact, he apol-
ogized to the fans for some of the things he had said.

Sometimes the men who broadcast for other teams and
have a pregame interview show can be helpful. You can
find out what players are good interviewees and what they
like to talk about. You can learn if a fellow is funny.
Some players are religious and enjoy talking about it on
the air, explaining what religion has meant to them in their
daily lives.

Once in a while an interviewer will come up with an idea
that he employs fairly regularly. For a while I used this one
with American League players: "If you were a fan, what
three players would you pay to see in the American
League?" The answers were varied and interesting, and the
particular year I used it, the players most mentioned were
Frank Howard, Carl Yastrzemski, Denny McLain, and Al
Kaline.

Sometimes I will ask a player on the air, "What was the
best question anyone ever asked you? The worst? The
silliest?" Then there's always the old reliable: "What was

your greatest thrill?" We try very hard to phrase this question in different ways, because it seems so mundane, but the truth is that every player has a different answer.

If I know a hitter well enough and I come up with the old one about who are the toughest pitchers in the league, I will tell him beforehand that I am going to ask him this question (which gives him time to think about his answer), and I ask him not to say, "Gosh Ken, they're all tough for me." Most of them will give you an honest reply.

The press books that are put out by the ball clubs, as well as any other reading material, can be invaluable. Features on players appear in publications like the *Sporting News, Sport* magazine, and *Sports Illustrated.* I often cut out these features and file them for future reference if they are about an athlete I am apt to interview.

In football a tough interview is one with a coach or player the week before a game. Most coaches have mastered the art of answering without really saying anything, and some can actually make it sound interesting. In the psychological warfare that is involved in football a coach will rarely, and then only inadvertently, make a derogatory comment about an opposing team or coach or player. He is not about to build any fires for the opposition. Invariably, he will heap them with praise.

At least, though, you can have a little fun with them. The week before the Browns-Colts N.F.L. championship game in 1964 I had Frank Ryan, the Browns quarterback, on the air. He is a brillant man with a dry sense of humor. I hit him with "Frank, what's your game plan for Sunday?" He paused, and came back with "Our game plan is to win."

A type of interview I enjoy very much is during a rain delay in a ball game. Sometimes you have to fill for forty or fifty minutes or so, and I believe strongly in keeping the mikes open at the ball park instead of sending back to the studio for music. For one thing, if someone tunes in and hears music, he may figure the game is off, or there is no game tonight and you have lost a listener. More important is the fact that you can get into some interesting discussions—with former players, a general manager, a visiting broadcaster (Bob Elson makes a tremendous guest), scout, newspaperman, etc.

People are under the impression, because of the time involved, that this is a difficult type of interview. It is not easy, but every time you run out of questions you can make a reference to the rain delay, how it looks right now, what the score is, and more or less regroup while you are doing this. If outside guests are not available, you can talk with your fellow broadcasters. Ned Martin and I have had some great chats with Mel Parnell and Johnny Pesky about baseball. There are other people who can be good too—for example, umpires and trainers.

I do a fifteen-minute interview before each Red Sox game on radio and about ten minutes before each game on TV, plus interviews for my daily show. I am always trying to come up with questions.

One good source is a player who you know is a good friend of the person you are going to interview. Sometimes he can give you some tips on what to ask. Buddy Leroux, the trainer of the Red Sox, has excellent rapport with the players. Jerry Moses, who once caught for Boston, was a very nice, very big, and, fortunately for me, very good-natured young man from Yazoo City, Mississippi. Somehow or other Leroux found out that Jerry had taken ballet lessons as a boy. Once on a live TV interview, right near the end, I said, "Jerry, I understand from Buddy Leroux that you took ballet lessons as a youngster. Do you feel that this has helped your footwork in catching?" Anyone looking in on a color TV set probably saw Jerry's face turn crimson, but he got a kick out of it and we had a good laugh.

One thing I really enjoy doing is bringing young boys from my town into the ball park to see a game on Saturday or Sunday. Especially if it's their first game. Sometimes I tell them who my guest is going to be on the pregame show and I will ask if they have any suggestions for questions. Once in a while they come up with some very good ones.

I like interview shows because it gives me a chance to ask people questions that I might not ask under ordinary circumstances and to learn more about them and the game they play. Any questions?

What was my toughest interview? They're all tough.

CHAPTER **10**

The Announcer
Wears Many Hats

Like an actor with a repertory company, an announcer must learn to play many roles. He does play-by-play, conducts interviews, and has a daily sports show, but in addition he may be called upon to deliver commercials, speak to clubs and "sports night" groups, emcee banquets, take part in community work, and entertain advertising clients.

The biggest problem he faces in all this is making sure that he is prepared for each of these difficult tasks and that he doesn't spread himself so thin that his work in any one area suffers.

The additional duties an announcer often assumes besides his play-by-play work and daily show can be a means of augmenting his income. Some announcers make personal appearances. The money earned will depend on how big a name the announcer is and how well he can handle a speaking engagement.

I take few of them. During the baseball season it is virtually impossible. We travel about ninety days during the season, plus five weeks of spring training. When the team is home, it plays almost every night during the week. On the evenings I am free, I prefer to spend time with my family.

Occasionally I make exceptions. For example, there is

one extra job I do with great pride, despite the time it takes. This is my involvement with the Jimmy Fund. Tom Yawkey, owner of the Red Sox, has been close to this most worthwhile endeavor for many years.

The Jimmy Fund is the name for the Children's Cancer Research Foundation, founded by the Variety Club of New England in 1947. The late Lou Perini, who owned the Boston Braves, was one of the founders, and Ted Williams has always been one of the fund's strongest boosters. Williams, in fact, is still honorary chairman, with Tom Yawkey chairman of the board, Dr. Sidney Farber the president, and Bill Koster the vice president and executive director.

I became general chairman in 1967, and in the next five years more than four million dollars was given to the fund, through appeals over the Red Sox baseball network and from general drives throughout New England.

The money comes in nickels and dimes and it comes in multithousand-dollar checks. People get a kick out of hearing their names over the air, so I acknowledge the contributions between innings of the games.

The ten-story Jimmy Fund building is located near Fenway Park and has 288 doctors caring for 600 children.

The Jimmy Fund appeal is possibly the biggest and most long-lasting drive in New England and the most popular, and I am proud to be associated with it. During the baseball season, about the only speaking dates I accept are in connection with the Jimmy Fund.

During the off season I take on a few other speaking dates. My presentation consists of telling a few funny stories along the way, answering questions, and relating some appropriate material. I prepare a completely different presentation for a father-son group than I would for a group of business executives.

Sometimes I'll serve as master of ceremonies at a sports

dinner. Each year in Manchester, New Hampshire, Leo Cloutier puts together one of the biggest sports banquets in the country, under the auspices of the Manchester *Union-Leader*.

A crowd of 2500 comes to the Manchester Armory to eat chicken pie and be entertained by a veritable "who's who in sports."

I have emceed this affair many times. With so many great athletes on the dais, my job is to keep my remarks to a minimum and make the program roll along quickly.

It is a most pleasant evening. I get to meet stars from the National League and from sports other than baseball —celebrities I don't encounter in my work with the Red Sox. If there is time I can tape interviews for my radio show. All this is good exposure for an announcer.

I started doing speaking engagements when I was twenty-one years old and working at WJDA in Quincy, Massachusetts. WJDA was about three months old when I joined the staff, and it was a daytime station. At night, we were expected to talk to groups in the broadcasting area to let people know there was a new station serving them.

It was good experience and I learned a great deal. I find that most people who have to speak in public share a common feeling: getting through the difficult period just before you actually get up to speak, usually when you are making polite talk over dessert.

This is when your hands get sweaty, your mind goes out of gear, and you wish you were home watching *The Dating Game* on television.

It's like a player going into a game. He's apprehensive until it starts, then he does his job. Once you're on your feet and get started it can be fun. Somebody once told me that the way to relax when giving a talk was to imagine that everyone in the audience was sitting there in his shorts.

I've never had to resort to that gimmick, but I do know that with experience you realize that the people out there are rooting for you and are receptive to what you have to say. The prespeech pressure will get less and less, but there will always be some. You should learn to live with it, and enjoy the dessert.

In public speaking, as in broadcasting, there will be good nights and bad nights. I've made some of my best speeches in the car on the way home, an hour after the dinner ended.

Bear in mind, too, that your basic business is broadcasting, and while you may be perfectly at home in front of a microphone, you simply might not be any good at public speaking. This is no crime. If you can evaluate yourself honestly in this area and find that public speaking is hurting your broadcasting image, cease and desist. We should all know our limitations.

During the season, it is customary for the sales staff of a radio and television station to bring clients to a ball game. The station usually rents a suite at a hotel near Fenway Park. At dinner, I am called upon to make a few remarks about the Red Sox and the show in general.

The entertaining is usually done before a night game and is set up several months in advance. I will tape my radio shows ahead so I can spend some time visiting with the clients. This type of affair takes place three or four times during the season and sometimes even after the season is over.

Attending these dinners is part of my job, and is often interesting because you get to meet the people who think enough of your work to invest in you.

When a salesman is attempting to sell your sports show, he will sometimes ask you to come along to meet the prospective client. I have done this, but with some reluctance. I am, after all, the product the salesman is trying to sell.

TO: Ken Coleman   Date: August 22, 1952
        Charles Hutaff
        Bill Dix
        Ed Leonard
        Norm Cloutier
        Bob Bouwsma
        Joe Bova
        Clem Scerback

From: Hamilton Shea   Subject: Browns Games

On Friday, August 29, at 3 p.m. Carling's and Lang, Fisher & Stashower are
conducting in Suite 316 of Hotel Hollenden a discussion of the plans for the
promotion of the Cleveland Browns broadcasts this year with the out-of-town
stations who will carry the games. This is an extremely important meeting
from the standpoint of the technical operation of the network and the joint
and individual promotion of the Cleveland Browns and the broadcast of their
games. The stations on the network will be represented by their chief executive and any other executives they choose to bring.

WTAM will play a prominent part in the agenda for the meeting, and the following assignments are hereby made:

    Hutaff: Prepare for my use in talking to the group an outline of
              the promotional plans originated and proposed by WTAM.
              This should be broken down into two sections - (1) promo-
              tions already started, and either completed or in process;
              (2) new promotions planned beyond the date of this meeting.
              You should be prepared with samples and blow-ups to supple-
              ment my discussion.

    Coleman: At the conclusion of my talk, I will introduce you to the
              gathering, and you will be counted on for appropriate
              remarks covering both your part in any promotional ventures
              we will undertake, and your plans for broadcasting the games.

    Leonard: You will be introduced by Bob Garretson of Carlings, and
              should be prepared to exhibit a map showing the network
              coverage for these games, and to discuss in general terms
              the arrangements for the network. At the conclusion of
              the prepared talk, questions will be invited from the floor
              for you to answer involving any details of the network trans-
              mission of the games.

The rest of the WTAM group will be present at these meetings and the social
events to follow mainly for public relations purposes, but you should all be
prepared to answer questions about our participation in the games and in the
promotion around them.

This is the first prominent occasion at which WTAM will be called on to prove
its exceptional ability to handle the Cleveland Browns football games, so I
want to urge everyone involved to take this assignment most seriously, to
appear on time, and to be prepared to answer all questions involving his own
individual participation in the venture.

There's more to broadcasting than simply turning up in the booth
at game time.

It is embarrassing to be present as the salesman extols my would-be virtues. I try to avoid the situation unless the salesman feels it is imperative I be there.

The interoffice memo on page 107 is an example of the sort of assignment I might get at a client meeting.

After a sale is made, however, particularly on the small- and medium-market level, it is important that you service the client. This means visiting his place of business, meeting the people who work there, and learning all you can about his product so you can sell it better on the air.

Sincerity is the most important factor in delivering a commercial. You must sound as though you care, that you personally have tried the product and find it worthwhile.

In the smaller market you may sometimes write the commercial as well as deliver it. In Cleveland, a major market, I was on the air for a number of years for a client who became a close personal friend. With the advertising agency's permission I wrote commercials because I knew the man and his business so well I was able to do the job.

To practice delivering commercials, you can write your own copy, borrow some from a local radio station, or read copy out of magazines and newspapers. The secret in reading properly is to sound as though you aren't reading. This is something that will come only through practice. You should spend many hours with a tape recorder to perfect your style.

Incidentally, the first time you hear yourself on a tape recorder will be a scary, and probably a depressing, experience. No matter how good your voice is, you are not going to believe that the sounds coming from the recorder are you.

If you make a tape with a friend, he will sound like him —but you won't sound like you. And he'll feel the same way, in reverse. This is a perfectly normal reaction. You will also find that when you listen to yourself you probably won't like what you hear. Most people are supercritical of their own performances. This should wear off with time and experience.

Boston, a great baseball city, has an organization called the Bosox Club, made up of about five hundred business executives who are interested in promoting the game.

They meet several times a year, mostly during the baseball season. Former ballplayers Dom DiMaggio and Ted Lepcio are past presidents of the group. Managers and players from both the Red Sox and visiting clubs are guests at these Bosox meetings. Generally I serve as master of ceremonies, as well as an interviewer.

Other major league cities have similar organizations, and on the road I am often asked to attend their meetings, along with the Red Sox manager and a couple of players. It is my job to interview them as part of the program.

Another job I sometimes take on is that of being a sports writer. For several years I wrote a column for the TV magazine section of the Sunday edition of the Boston *Herald-Traveler*. I have also written occasional pieces for other publications.

Personally, the most important hat I wear is one most men share with me—that of husband and father. In the broadcasting business, there are the usual plusses and minuses for a family—but the traveling sometimes makes it difficult for us to be together for long periods.

I take my wife Ellen and at least a couple of the children (we have five) to part of spring training. My wife also makes several trips with me during the regular season.

My family often gets to meet celebrities, which is fun for them. I suppose being around sports figures so much has added to my childrens' interest in sports, although this, too, has its drawbacks.

I've often watched a father and his boy at the ball park, eager and excited over the prospect of seeing a major league ball game. Because my children and I see so many games, a day at Fenway is no longer a novelty for us. The treat is for those who see only a couple of games a season.

Still, I know my children have enjoyed their sports exposure. My oldest son, Casey, worked for several years at the Cleveland Browns camp helping trainer Leo Murphy and equipment manager Morrie Kono. Casey later became a good high school quarterback and was outstanding in prep school, perhaps because he had a chance to work out with professionals like Frank Ryan and Jim Ninowski.

Billy, the youngest, has a famous godfather, Lou Groza, the great place-kicker of the Browns. Once Billy stole the show in a father-and-son game with the Cleveland Indians. He hit safely, turned first, headed for second and kept right on going into left field, with Tito Francona in hot pursuit.

My oldest daughter, Kerry, was an outstanding swimmer in Cohasset, Massachusetts. Kathleen was a catcher in softball and a goaltender in field hockey and is interested in becoming a physical education teacher. And youngest daughter Susan? Well, she's just a knowledgeable, all-around fan who thinks Curt Gowdy is a terrific announcer.

As I mentioned, one of the biggest drawbacks to the job is the time I spend away from home. This is when I feel I'm really earning my money. My wife has to take on the added responsibility of being a father as well as a mother.

Once the baseball season begins, I work long hours, seven days a week even when the club is at home. There is little time for social life. However, during the off season, I am home more than most men. I do my programs in the afternoon and am home most nights by seven o'clock.

So, as in every line of work, there are good things and bad. If you go into broadcasting with your eyes open, you'll be aware of the bad parts. You'll know whether you can put up with the traveling, with the tension and the practice.

You'll judge for yourself how many hats you can wear and still be comfortable.

CHAPTER 11

The Role of the Former Athlete

Columnist Jim Murray defined the ex-ballplayer turned broadcaster as a man whose main accomplishment was getting three hits in ten times at bat, replacing someone who has spent twenty-five years sweeping floors, doing commercials, and otherwise learning his craft.

This is a harsh and simplified definition, but even if it were true it is beside the point, because the ex-player is in the broadcasting booth to stay. A former athlete has as much right to be in the announcing business as anyone else.

He should not be resented merely because he once played the game proficiently and has not had to spend an apprenticeship in his new field. His apprenticeship was in the hundreds of games he played, which should have given him an insight into the sport and those who played it.

The resentment should come, however, if the ex-player does not do his announcing job well—if his playing experience hinders rather than helps him.

Then the big name should be resented, not only by his fellow announcers but also by the fans who are forced to put up with his incompetence.

More and more professional athletes are entering the broadcasting field. They used to get into the radio end of the game almost by accident. A big-name player would re- tire and either a ball club or a network would give him a try in the booth. Among the early stars who were success- ful as baseball play-by-play announcers were Jack Graney with the Indians (as a player he got the first hit off a nine- teen-year-old pitcher named Babe Ruth), Harry Heilman with the Tigers, and Waite Hoyt with the Reds.

I've talked with a number of athletes who have been considering sports announcing as a career when their play- ing days are over. A couple of years ago, Jim Price, who was a player representative with the Tigers, brought a tape recorder to the winter meetings so that he could interview athletes for his winter sports show back home.

During the 1971 season, Baltimore Orioles announcer Chuck Thompson told me that Pete Richert, who was then a reliever with the club, was interested in becoming an announcer. Richert would often sit with Thompson and associate Bill O'Donnell and discuss techniques.

The majority of ex-players in the booth are color men, or analysts, although many have gone on to do the more demanding play-by-play portion. Frank Gifford, Phil Riz- zuto, George Kell, Herb Score, and the late Paul Christman are a few who come to mind.

Bud Blattner, who does the Kansas City Royals baseball broadcasts, is a very polished performer and has done other sports, basketball in particular, very capably. There isn't much call for table tennis announcers, but Bud is an expert there too, being a former champion.

Johnny Pesky, who works with Ned Martin and me on Red Sox baseball, is primarily a color man. He's especially good during rain delays, when we can reminisce about the old days. Mel Parnell, his predecessor, was also good at flashbacks.

Pesky and Parnell and most of those who step from the field to the microphone are not professional announcers and shouldn't try to be. They should be themselves. What they contribute is a knowledge of the game and what it's like to be a big leaguer.

Unfortunately, the very thing that makes a player an expert about a sport can inhibit him in his broadcasting work. Too often, especially when he's just breaking into broadcasting, the former player takes an athlete's view of every situation. He still thinks of himself as part of the fraternity, so to speak.

Thus, if an outfielder misplays a ball, the ex-player is apt to make an excuse for him, because he knows the feeling that comes from booting one. Many athletes are not as objective as they might be when describing a play, but with experience the good ones loosen up.

I've worked alongside some great athletes. In Cleveland, quarterback Otto Graham was my color man one year, and for many seasons I teamed with the late Warren Lahr, who was an outstanding cornerback with the Browns for eleven years. Nationally, I've been with Frank Gifford, Tom Brookshier, Gordie Soltau, Don Paul, Pat Summerall, Red Grange, Dave Kocourek, and Johnny Morris.

I seemed to work best with Gifford and Summerall. What I liked about them (and I give Summerall the edge here) is that they did not attempt to come in with a comment after every play. They were smart enough to step in when they had something pertinent, say it, and then step out.

The list of athletes turned announcers is growing and growing. Here are some others who have gone from the field to the booth in recent years: Joe Nuxhaul, Al Derogatis, Willie Davis, Rocky Colavito, Bill White, Jack Twyman, Elgin Baylor, Hot Rod Hundley, Bill Russell, Nellie

King, Jerry Coleman, George Kell, Don Hoak, George Ratterman, Paul Maguire, and Don Drysdale.

Even though a player may have seemed the epitome of coolness as he stood on the mound with the bases loaded and, say, Harmon Killebrew at bat, he is often not prepared for the pressures of the broadcasting booth. There is quite an adjustment, and men who have played under pressure for many years have told me they feel the tension just as much, and sometimes more, in broadcasting.

The average sports announcer spent years in the minor leagues of broadcasting, working all phases of the business. He's as much at home at the mike as the player was with a bat or on the pitching mound.

When the broadcaster moved to the big leagues, he was familiar with the techniques and the equipment. But the player goes from the field to the booth without that preparation.

Most former players have never scored a game. They have no idea of how to conduct an interview. They've been interviewed many times themselves, but that's another ball game altogether. So is providing color commentary. We used to kid Mel Parnell, and later Johnny Pesky, both of whom are great storytellers. They'd start recounting a story of the old Red Sox days while we were on an airplane or on the bus to the park, and we'd tell them to save it for the ball game.

Many color men have trouble telling anecdotes on the air. They are too stiff and formal, even though their off-mike delivery is easy. They have a preconceived notion of how they should act when on.

Some players catch on quickly. Tony Kubek, the former Yankee infielder, works with Curt Gowdy on *The Game of the Week* and has done well right from the start. Sandy Koufax, on the other hand, got off to the same slow start in broadcasting as he did as a pitcher. It took Koufax about five years to blossom into the Hall of Fame pitcher he became.

His work on *The Game of the Week* has been getting better each year. It might be hard for the average fan to realize, but a man can be an aggressive, dominant figure on the field and a quiet, shy person away from it. I worked with Koufax in 1967, found him likable and personable and the possessor of a fine voice.

He is basically shy, a perfectly good quality but an inhibiting one in front of a mike. Broadcasting and telecasting are, let's face it, a form of show business. Many actors and comedians come on strong when they're working but are introverted away from the stage.

Probably the best way for an athlete who wants to eventually get his foot in the door is simply to make his feelings known, the way Pete Richert has.

The athlete also has an entree to the front office that few others have—and to the radio and TV stations as well. The player is already a celebrity in his own right.

A broadcast executive can usually tell five minutes after the player sits down whether he has the potential to make it someday as a big-league announcer.

Because a former player was a member of the lodge, he is sometimes privy to information that some announcers cannot get, simply because he knows the players well. A veteran broadcaster gets to know plenty of players, but it takes time to gain their confidence.

More and more professional athletes are college graduates—articulate, poised, and intelligent. They are becoming aware that sports broadcasting is a good way to make a living.

However, there will always be a place in announcing for the talented nonathlete, or for the one whose greatest claim to athletic fame was the day he pitched a shutout for North Quincy High.

CHAPTER 12

Producing and Directing

Harry Jones, the Cleveland Indians telecaster, was sitting in the dugout at Tiger Stadium in Detroit, about an hour and a half before the start of a night game. Russ Schneider, baseball writer for the Cleveland *Plain Dealer*, came by and asked Harry if the game was being televised back to Cleveland.

Harry replied yes, they were sending the game back, and this was a makeup game to replace an earlier one that had been rained out. Then Schneider came in with an interesting observation.

"How," he asked, "are you going to televise if you don't have any cameras?"

Jones, who had just arrived in the park, looked around and there wasn't a camera in sight. He immediately called the station in Cleveland, to discover that the men with the answers were all at the annual company picnic.

In the decision to televise this game, one executive was under the impression that another was making the arrangements, and vice versa. There was no baseball televised to Cleveland that night.

This admittedly rare failure in interoffice communications would never have happened if Harry Jones had had a producer with him. On the network level, a producer is

This is what the control room looks like at Cleveland's Municipal Stadium. *Photo by Beacon (Ohio)* Journal

always on hand, and on our Red Sox telecasts we have a man—Roger Shea—who acts as producer on the road and as combination producer-director at home.

The producer is responsible for all aspects of the event. He coordinates all elements of a pickup. He makes arrangements to have a crew available for road games, sets up the broadcast lines, makes sure the monitors are in the right place, coordinates the telecast with the playing of the national anthem, finds out whether there will be any special pregame activities and whether they should be televised, and even determines such basics as the starting time of the game itself.

The director has one prime function—to give the viewer the best visual presentation of the game. Perhaps more than the producer, he must have a working knowledge of the sport so he can anticipate game situations. Ideally it is best if both men have a knowledge and feel for the game.

Roger Shea is such a man and does such a good job that viewers take it for granted that they'll see the best presentation of the action. One of Shea's rare mistakes, in early 1972, gave baseball fans an idea of how important a director is. Red Sox pitcher Ray Culp was an out away from a 1 to 0 shutout of the Brewers in Milwaukee when catcher Daryl Porter slammed a long drive to right.

The usual directorial move here is to follow the right fielder with the camera as he drifts toward the fence, thus zeroing in on the potential home run.

But Shea, in the broadcasting truck, didn't direct the camera to switch from Culp to right fielder Reggie Smith. As the ball glanced off the leaping Smith's glove into the stands for game-tying homer, the picture at home showed Culp looking toward the outfield and then putting his hands on his hips in dejection.

"When people ask me about it," said Shea, "I tell them I wanted to give the fans a different view of what happened, but the truth is I just blew the shot." For Roger, it was a once-in-a-lifetime goof.

Let's use a baseball game as an example to show how the announcer relates to the producer and director. We televise about sixty games a season, so we don't have a meeting before each game, but we do get together periodically, and always have a meeting prior to the start of the season. Shea conducts the session, and he might say something like this:

"Ken is on the play-by-play and Johnny [Pesky] will do the color. We'll have a five-minute pregame show. Ken will open, set the stage and throw Johnny a question or two.

Throw the cue to commercial about a minute and a half in. The cue is, 'We'll be back with the starting lineups in just a moment.'

"Ken will pick it up after the spot and give the lineups, finishing with the pitchers. We'll get a shot of the pitchers as he goes over their records, shooting the Red Sox pitcher first. Then comes the closing cue, and we'll return after the opening billboard for the game. Some of the stations won't be carrying the pregame show, so reestablish the scene when you come on at the opening of the game.

"After the anthem, throw the cue for the first commercial. There'll be a commercial after each half inning. At the end of the fifth and seventh, there'll be a ninety-second spot, so give us a very fast cue at the end of those innings. There will also be a commercial cue when there is a pitching change. Station breaks will be given each hour and the A.D. [associate director] will handle the card. John will handle the instant replays."

As you can see, Roger has covered a lot of ground. When he is directing, he communicates with us in the booth from his spot in the mobile unit. The associate director, also called the stage manager or floor man, has a series of cards, which he will hand us to read at the appropriate times.

The cards include such information as the disclaimer, "This broadcast is authorized by the Boston Red Sox solely for the entertainment of our listening audience. Any rebroadcast or other use of the pictures, description and accounts of this game without the express written consent of the Boston Red Sox is prohibited."

The A.D. will also have cards (at least, in our system) marked "instant replay," "slow motion," and "back live." Sometimes, if we want a particular shot, we will whisper to the A.D., who will relay the request to Roger in the truck. The communication is quick and to the point. I may be on the air and Roger will say into my earpiece, "on deck." I then know that as soon as I finish he will take a shot of the man in the on-deck circle. Occasionally I will keep on talking and he will shoot the man in the circle. The decision to comment on the player is mine. There is no hard and fast rule in this area.

I've had the pleasure of working with such top directors as Harry Coyle at NBC, Bob Dailey and Tony Verna at CBS, Jack Simon, Clay Dopp, and Joe O'Rourke at the Hughes Sports Network, and many others on a regional basis, such as Shea and Tony Lolli in Cleveland. These men are qualified, competent professionals, and they, along with the cameramen and other technicians, can really make or break a televised sporting event.

The ones I've mentioned here have one trait in common, a trait that is mandatory for anyone that's good in our business. They are cool under pressure. Once in awhile something goes wrong during a telecast, such as a shot missed by a cameraman because of a technical problem over which he has no immediate control. I have had the misfortune of working with directors and producers who react like a wounded buffalo when they get into this sort of situation, which only compounds the problem.

The most important thing to remember in working with producers and directors is that you are part of a team. Sometimes they will make suggestions that can enhance the quality of the broadcast. Sometimes you may want to ask them to cover an unusual aspect of the game. You should always remember that the job they are doing is every bit as important as yours. You are the recognizable face and voice, but the quality of the telecast will depend pretty much on how well these men behind the scenes do their jobs.

The director must have a definite approach, a theory on

how to handle the game. A good director gives a fan a box-seat view of the game. A bad one puts a viewer behind a post.

Too many cameras are often as bad as not enough. This can disrupt directional continuity, and there is a tendency to overuse cameras. A director must use judgment and restraint.

This book is directed primarily toward sports broadcasting. Production and direction, though obviously a part of broadcasting, are another specialty. But as a sportscaster you have to understand these men and their problems as you work with them. They are, after all, on your side.

CHAPTER **13**

Well-known Announcers and How They Got That Way

The term well-known, as used here, is relative. A sports announcer can be well known regionally or nationally. Bob Neal, for example, is well known in Cleveland; Dick Enberg and Don Wells are well known on the West Coast. Gene Elston is familiar to Texans, Milo Hamilton to Georgians, Ernie Harwell to Michiganders. There are other men who are known around the country because they work on network assignments most of the time.

Here are the capsule stories of some regional and national broadcasters and how they worked their way up to the major leagues of sport.

CURT GOWDY was a fine basketball player at the University of Wyoming, but a back injury cut short his career. He went to work reporting high school sports for a newspaper in Cheyenne, where he grew up. He used to broadcast games for fun and practice in his room at home, using his imagination.

Gowdy had been discharged from the Army because of the back condition, and when an opening came up at the local radio station, he got the job. He covered all kinds of events around Cheyenne and after a year was assigned to do the University of Oklahoma games. One day, Red Barber, then sports director at CBS in New York, assigned him to the Oklahoma-Texas Christian football game.

His work on that game gained him national attention, and soon after he was hired by the New York Yankees as the number two man to Mel Allen. A few years later he became the Red Sox play-by-play specialist, and in 1966 he left for a network job. Gowdy, with color man Paul Christman, was the television voice of the American Football League from its inception to the pro football merger. In 1970 he received the Peabody Award for highest achievement in radio and television, the only man from the field of sports to receive this award. Gowdy has covered more major events than anyone else in the history of sports broadcasting.

CHRIS SCHENKEL started broadcasting in the area around his hometown, Bippus, Indiana, covering the high school basketball games. He majored in radio broadcasting at Purdue and covered the college games for small local stations in Indiana. He served as track announcer at Lincoln Downs, in Rhode Island, before his first big break in 1952, when he was signed to do the New York Giants football games, a one-year assignment that lasted for thirteen seasons. For the last several years he's handled major sports events for ABC and its *Wide World of Sports*. This includes the top college football games, the Olympic Games, the Masters, the U.S. Open and other major golf tournaments, and N.B.A. basketball.

VIN SCULLY, strangely enough, was a New York Giants baseball fan as a youngster. The voice of the Dodgers grew up in New York and started broadcasting at Fordham University. He worked as a staff announcer for WTOP in

Washington, D.C., and went from there to Brooklyn as the third man on Dodgers games. Scully has been with the Dodgers ever since, and restricts his activities to describing their games. He's probably received more critical acclaim as a day-in, day-out baseball broadcaster than any other man in the profession.

JIM SIMPSON started his career at the age of fifteen on a tiny station, WINX, in Washington, D.C. His first big break came while in the Navy in 1952. Stationed in Finland, Simpson was asked by CBS to broadcast special reports on the Olympics, which were being held in Helsinki. The next year, after getting out of the service, Simpson went to work for a television station in Washington, D.C. In 1960, he joined ABC, teaming up with Jim McKay on the network's prizewinning show, *Wide World of Sports.* In 1964, he moved to NBC, where today he is considered one of the nation's finest sportscasters. Since going to NBC, Simpson has broadcast everything from baseball and football to the Winter Olympics and Wimbledon tennis.

LINDSEY NELSON's career began while he was attending the University of Tennessee, where he did the school's football games. In 1951 he was hired by Liberty Broadcasting to air both baseball and football. The next year, he switched to NBC, where for ten years he was one of the dominant sports voices in America. In 1962, he hooked up with the newly created New York Mets as their radio and TV man, chronicling their early disasters and their later triumphs. He has continued throughout his career to do N.C.A.A. football in the fall.

RAY SCOTT went to work for a small radio station in his hometown, Johnstown, Pennsylvania, for a salary of fifty-five dollars a month. This was in 1937. His job consisted of announcing, writing copy, selling advertising, and also doing some janitorial chores. After serving in the Army during World War II, Ray went to work for station WCAE in Pittsburgh, where he also broadcast Carnegie Tech football games in his free time. Scott left broadcasting shortly afterward to work for an advertising agency, but also did some freelance announcing. With the advent of television, Ray returned to the broadcasting world, doing N.F.L. games over the Dumont Television Network in 1953.

In 1956, he was assigned to the Sugar Bowl game with Bill Stern, then considered tops in the business. Stern became ill at the start of the game and Scott had to do all the announcing. His fine job won for him the Green Bay Packers assignment over CBS television that same season. Scott still does N.F.L. games for CBS, including the Super Bowl. He is also associated with the Hughes Sports Network, covering major college basketball games and various golf tournaments.

DON DUNPHY and boxing are synonymous. In the 1940's and 50's when boxing was at its peak, he was one of the prime voices in bringing the excitement of the top bouts to millions of listeners. Don attended Manhattan College in New York, and after graduation worked part time for the New York *Journal* and the New York *World-Telegram*.

Don first became involved in the fight game as a public relations director of the old New York Coliseum, in the Bronx. As his knowledge of boxing grew, he went to work for radio station WINS, where he might broadcast as many as twenty-four three-round matches in a single night.

His big opportunity came in 1941 when Don won an audition to broadcast the Joe Louis-Billy Conn heavyweight championship fight. From then on, Don Dunphy was identified with the best in boxing broadcasting. However, he was not just a one-sport announcer. He's done everything from the World Series to bowling matches.

JACK BRICKHOUSE, broadcaster of the Chicago Cubs, was born in Peoria, Illinois, and attended Bradley University. He always wanted to be a broadcaster, so one day he entered a contest sponsored by the Peoria radio station. There were six finalists and four prizes. He finished fifth. But he got a job at the radio station anyway.

Those early days were a struggle for Brickhouse: he constantly found himself trying to imitate the styles of the big-name broadcasters. Finally he took the advice of a fellow announcer, relaxed at the mike, and stopped trying to sound like other people. His identity established, Brickhouse soon went to work as a sportscaster for both the White Sox and the Cubs in Chicago. Today he confines himself to televising about 150 Cubs games a year.

MARV ALBERT, broadcaster of Knicks basketball and Rangers hockey in New York City, first became involved with sports at fourteen, when he worked as an office boy for the Brooklyn Dodgers and as a ball boy for the Knicks. He attended Syracuse University and started his career at station WFBL, doing Syracuse baseball games and disc jockey work. One of the brightest young voices in the profession, Marv has two younger brothers who are also sports announcers. Al Albert is the voice of the New York Nets, of the American Basketball Association. The youngest brother, Steve, has handled some play-by-play for the Springfield Kings, an American Hockey League team.

DAN KELLY, who has done CBS's *Hockey Game of the Week,* in addition to being the voice of the St. Louis Blues Hockey Club, followed his older brother, Hal, into sportscasting. A graduate of St. Patrick's College in Ottawa,

Canada, Kelly won an audition to broadcast the games of the Canadian Football League, a job he handled for four years. In 1967 he was named for the St. Louis Blues assignment.

MARTY GLICKMAN was one of the first of the athletes to become a broadcaster. Born in Brooklyn, Marty was a standout athlete—a sprinter and football player—at James Madison High and then at Syracuse University. He was a member of the United States track team in the 1936 Olympics in Berlin. Glickman's broadcasting career started while he was an undergraduate at Syracuse. After graduation he went on to play pro football, but continued his broadcasting career, working for station WHN in New York.

In 1948, Marty became the radio play-by-play announcer for the New York Football Giants, a position he still holds. Glickman has covered just about every sport imaginable, and was probably the first of the colorful basketball announcers, doing the early Knicks as well as college games.

FRANK GIFFORD is another athlete who has made the transition from the playing fields to the broadcast booth. An All-American halfback at the University of Southern California, Gifford starred for twelve seasons with the New York Giants. During his career he set several Giant team records and in 1956 was voted the N.F.L.'s Most Valuable Player.

Frank's sportscasting career actually began at CBS radio in 1961, when he was still a member of the Giants. After retiring from football in 1964, Gifford went to work as a color man on N.F.L. telecasts for CBS. In 1971, he switched to ABC, this time as a play-by-play announcer on ABC's Monday Night Football.

ERNIE HARWELL started his career in sports when he was fifteen, working as a correspondent for the Atlanta *Constitution* and the *Sporting News*. He moved into broadcasting in 1940 at station WSB in his hometown of Atlanta. After the Second World War, Harwell started broadcasting the baseball games of the Atlanta Crackers, of the Southern Association. In 1948 he moved to the majors to team with Red Barber on the Brooklyn Dodgers broadcasts. A year later, Harwell went across town to work alongside Russ Hodges on the Giants games.

Ernie switched to the American League in 1954 as the broadcaster for the Baltimore Orioles. He also worked the Baltimore Colts football games. After six years in Baltimore, Harwell went to Detroit to become the voice of the Tigers, a position he's held for more than a decade.

Ernie can always tell people he was a broadcaster who once was traded for a ballplayer. This happened during his days with the Dodgers, when Branch Rickey was the team's general manager. Red Barber, the Dodgers announcer, was sick, and Rickey needed a replacement in a hurry. Harwell was in Atlanta at the time, so Rickey traded a minor leaguer to the Crackers for Ernie's services.

CHUCK THOMPSON is another who started his career while still in high school—working at station WRAW, a 250-watter in Reading, Pennsylvania. Chuck's career was interrupted by World War II. Upon returning home, he met John B. Kelly, father of former movie actress Grace Kelly, now Princess Grace of Monaco. Kelly, a big man in horse racing, asked Chuck to broadcast racing in Florida. Not long afterward, Chuck received a chance to do big league games with the Phillies and the Athletics. In 1949, he moved to Baltimore to handle both the Colts and the baseball Orioles, then a minor league team. After a stint in Washington as the Senator's broadcaster, he returned to Baltimore in 1961 as the voice of the now major league Orioles. An expert football man, Chuck has been a member of CBS's national staff in the telecasting of N.F.L. games for many years.

BOB PRINCE, the entertaining and controversial announcer for the Pittsburgh Pirates, had probably the oddest way of breaking into the industry. Prince answered a newspaper ad looking for a sportscaster. He took the job, which required him to do a fifteen-minute sports report daily for the magnificent sum of $7.50 a week.

MERLE HARMON started at a tiny station in Colorado. His first sportscasting job was describing the games of the Topeka Owls, a minor league baseball team. He did it from the studio from material that came across a Western Union ticker tape. Since then, he has done the games of the Kansas City Athletics, the Milwaukee Braves, and the Minnesota Twins and is currently doing the Milwaukee Brewers and the New York Jets football team.

HARRY KALAS and AL MICHAELS have this in common: They prepped in Hawaii, where there are no major league franchises yet but where there will be some one day. Kalas started by broadcasting the games of the Hawaii Islanders, of the Pacific Coast League. He later graduated to the Houston Astros, and is now broadcasting for the Philadelphia Phillies, along with BYRON SAAM, voice of the Phils since 1938, and RICHIE ASHBURN, the former outfielder.

Al Michaels also broke in by doing the games of the Islanders. In 1971, the Cincinnati Reds hired Michaels for their broadcasts. Within a year, the young man was doing special coverage assignments for NBC, including the 1972 Winter Olympics.

JOE GARAGIOLA is one athlete turned announcer who has really hit the jackpot. Joe's first break was doing the *Major League Game of the Week*. He later became play-by-play announcer for the Yankees, but he didn't stop there. He left the Yankees to join the *Today* show and to host his own quiz program.

TOM HARMON won the Heisman Trophy as an All-America back at the University of Michigan in 1940. He played pro football briefly with the Rams, but found his vocation when he turned to sportscasting. He's covered a variety of sports, and included in his big moments is the time he announced to the world that Sandy Koufax, the Dodgers' great left-hander, was retiring from baseball.

BUD PALMER is another former athlete. Palmer was a basketball player at Princeton and later with the New York Knicks. He first came to the attention of the viewing public when, oddly enough, he broadcast some hockey games in the 1950's. One of the highlights of his career came during the 1964 U.S. Open. He was at the microphone when Ken Venturi overcame heat prostration on the final day to win the championship.

DANNY GALLIVAN, the voice of the Montreal Canadiens, worked for a small station in Nova Scotia, announcing junior hockey games. He went to the Montreal Forum to do the play-by-play of the junior team he was covering, and an official of the Canadiens happened to catch the broadcast. He liked what he heard, and remembered the name, and a few years later, when the Canadiens were looking for someone to handle their play-by-play, Gallivan got the job.

JIM WOODS, who does the Oakland Athletics games, has

worked with some great announcers. Woods came to the majors when he joined Mel Allen on the Yankee broadcasts. Allen, who has been responsible for giving a number of sportscasters their start in the big leagues, demanded nothing less than 100 percent of his fellow announcers. Woods felt this training helped him become a better sportscaster. He later worked at Pittsburgh with another giant of the industry, Bob Prince, and after a year with the Cardinals he joined forces with Monte Moore at Oakland.

HARRY JONES was once a writer with the Cleveland *Plain Dealer*, covering the Indians games. He'd never done any radio or television work, but when TV became a bigger factor in major league baseball, Jones got into the picture. He's been the telecaster for Indians games for many years, the last several seasons with former pitcher Herb Score.

HOWARD COSELL has had more impact on the industry in recent years than any other sportscaster. He attended New York University and became a lawyer, and at twenty-one was admitted to the bar. Although he was successful, Howard admits he never really wanted to become a lawyer but did so because his father wanted his son to become a professional man.

Cosell came into the broadcasting industry when ABC Radio asked him to host a show in which Little Leaguers would question pro baseball players. Cosell at the time was legal counsel for Little League Baseball in New York. That show featuring Little Leaguers lasted five years.

In 1956, ABC offered Cosell a professional contract to do ten weekend sports shows of five minutes each. Cosell moved to television in 1961, joining ABC-TV in New York. His interviews with heavyweight champion Muhammad Ali and his self-named "tell it like it is" style thrust him into national prominence. He came into further national focus when ABC gave him the Monday Night N.F.L. football assignment.

DICK ENBERG started his career by accident. He was attending Central Michigan University when he applied for a janitor's job at a local radio station. Dick was told he could sweep the floors if he wanted to, but that he also would have to do some work as a disc jockey. Later, while working for his master's degree at the University of Indiana, he covered sports for the school's radio station. Today he is the voice of the California Angels and Rams football on radio, and also does U.C.L.A. games and major college basketball contests on television. Enberg also hosts a television quiz show, *The Sports Challenge*, which is syndicated and is seen on some 140 stations.

DON WELLS started his career after returning from the service in 1945. Working for a station in Salinas, California, Don broadcast games in the Sunset League. Just like a ballplayer, he moved through the ranks, working next in Wichita, a Class A city. Then he went to Dallas to broadcast the games of the Double A baseball club in that city. In 1952, Wells worked for the Liberty Broadcasting System and in 1953 was Bob Elson's partner in the White Sox radio booth. Don is now one of the broadcasters of Angels games, having returned to the West Coast when the team was formed in 1961.

BILL WHITE represents one of the major breakthroughs in sportscasting. A former ballplayer, Bill began to think about a career in radio and TV after Harry Caray, the Cardinals announcer when White played in St. Louis, suggested it. Near the end of his career with the Phillies, Bill replaced Dick Stuart on a show in Philadelphia. He became sports director of Philadelphia's WFIL before moving on to the Yankees as the first black play-by-play announcer.

The names in this chapter are obviously not all the announcers who have become well known in sports, either nationally or regionally. The list is endless.

But the point is, no two stories are alike. Each man got his big break in a different way and they all have had to work hard to stay at the top.

CHAPTER 14

Bouquets and Brickbats

I've done plenty of speaking before live audiences and even had one brief fling at summer stock, and I can say that talking to an unseen audience is an entirely different experience. As an announcer, virtually your only contact with the public is through letters from listeners.

I get a lot of mail, much of it from contributors to the Jimmy Fund, with appreciative notes about our broadcasting crew. I get a few hate letters from the kind of person who dislikes me because I mention that a player happens to be a nice guy and also happens to have black skin.

I've received letters referring to a specific broadcast in which I have been informed that I did a good job, and others referring to the same broadcast that said I was terrible. The first ones charged me with being strictly for the home team and the others chastised me for giving too much credit to the opposition.

This does not put me in any special category. Other sportscasters get similar letters.

I try to answer every letter that is signed. If it is not signed it hits the wastebasket immediately. If the letter is in the hate category, there is no point in trying to give a logical answer.

Some letters offer constructive criticism. A broadcaster sometimes falls into a pattern where he unconsciously overuses a word or phrase. A listener might notice this, let the announcer know, and help break what could be an annoying habit.

The vast majority of listeners don't write at all. Most who do write in do so because you have evoked in them strong emotions. They think you are great or they think you are terrible. Sometimes they are just plain thoughtful. These people will sit down at the end of a season and just drop a line to tell you they've enjoyed the year.

With all the praise and condemnation, the cheers and boos, where does this leave the announcer? Hopefully, with his feet planted solidly, accepting himself for what he is. It should also leave him never quite satisfied professionally, so that he tries to make the next broadcast the best one yet.

Here are some bouquets and brickbats typical of the ones I've received over the years:

Sometimes an announcer has to do what he is told by the station. This card came after we televised a baseball game on the Saturday the Kentucky Derby was being run. Because the game ran long, we were instructed to break in and announce the Derby winner.

K. Coleman, N. Martin and M. Parnell:
Thanks for spoiling the Derby for me this year. It is one of the sports thrills of the year, but not much fun when you know the winner. Why don't you three big mouths shut up now and then.
                              C. D. D.
                    Needham, Massachusetts

Here is the kind that makes you want to come back:

Dear Ken:
As a Red Sox fan of many years, I thought I would just drop you a note to say what a wonderful job you do as the

Red Sox number one announcer. I have listened to all the good announcers in both hockey and baseball over the last twenty-five years. You are not in hockey but you are terrific in baseball.

The way you handled the Petrocelli incident was beautiful. You didn't shy away from it, and you didn't present just one side of it. The fact that you brought it up when you have to be approved of by the Sox to do their games is a plus for you and the organization. You are a pleasure to listen to and I had a few minutes this morning so I thought I would tell you.

Sincerely,
J. C.
Burlington, Vermont

Dear Ken, Ned and Johnny:

I have invited you three guys into my home via radio and TV for every Red Sox game this season and I just want to say how much I've enjoyed your company. After Wednesday it will seem as if part of my family is gone away. Have a nice winter. We will look forward to next season.

A devoted Red Sox fan
from Marion, Massachusetts

And here's the kind that makes you want to take a vacation. This was a letter to Maurice Van Metre, who conducted the "Grins and Groans" column in the now defunct Cleveland *News*:

Dear Van:

The most horrible broadcast of a football game I ever heard was Ken Coleman's description of the Browns-49ers game on Sunday. He didn't know what the score was when it was 12 to 7 in favor of Cleveland. He said if Groza's

*kick was good it would be 14 to 7. He didn't know what
down it was half the time.*

*He said when the Browns had been penalized for too
many men on the field that the penalty was for an illegal
forward lateral. He continually chatted too much. He was
still talking when a play was run and then had to go back
and tell what happened. Certainly NBC can get someone
who knows a little about football. Personally, I think Coleman should pay his way to see the games.*

*J. W. C.
Euclid, Ohio*

And to think I spent two years in India in World War II!

Dear Mr. Coleman:

*As a nightly listener to your sports broadcast over
WHDH I humbly submit a suggestion relative to the prononciation of the word "bengal." I've noticed that you have
recently been referring to the Cincinnati Bengles. Just
to check, I looked it up in Webster's and the prononciation
given therein is "ben-gol" or "ben-gawl".*

*When the Tigers play the Red Sox I have heard them
referred to as the Bengals with the prononciation accord-
ing to Webster. And if I may say so, I do think the Webster
prononciation sounds much more ferocious and "tigerish."
The "bengle" sounds too harmless, more like an ornament
such as a bangle.*

*But whether it is "bengles" or "ben-gols", I do enjoy your
broadcasts and being a baseball fan above all other sports,
I am looking forward to next season and your broadcasts.*

*Very truly yours,
Mrs. I. S. W.
Boston,   Massachusetts*

All the time I thought I was telling it like it is, but a columnist in a newspaper in Maine thought otherwise. Here are some excerpts . . .

"I love the baseball broadcasters. I love them for their weaknesses. If they didn't violate the basic rules of news reporting they wouldn't command this absolute of love.

"I'm glad they're not impartial. If they were, we listeners would lose a great deal of poetry when the Red Sox were winning and many outraged expressions of unbelief when the team is being clobbered. . . .

"I often tune in when the games are more than half finished. I don't have to wait to hear the score announced. I can tell from the vocal lilt, or lack of it, whether or not it is a good night for Boston. . . .

"I tried one night with a piece of graph paper to chart Ken Coleman's enthusiasm variations, but I had to give up. The zooms and the dips ran right off the margins. It's either sunshine, roses, and sirloin steak for Ken, or it's dreary rain, skunk cabbage, and sour pea soup. . . .

"I hope the Red Sox announcers never become satiated and calm because if they do they'll take much joy from my life. . . ."

I think the gentleman that follows wants me to shut up:

Dear Sir:

You spoil the TV telecast and we enjoy the radio. Too much history and things about the past that you read from the record book.

You talk too much. Too much talk. We can see the game. I get tired of hearing you ask Pesky a damn fool question and a damn fool answer. You should hear him stumbling and stammering trying to explain a point.

We like the radio. Don't talk so much. I repeat, don't talk so much.

                              J. M.
                              Beverly, Massachusetts

When you do Harvard football you had better watch your grammar:

Dear Mr. Coleman:
We enjoy your play-by-play of Red Sox and Harvard games very much. However you make a very bad mistake in English many many times and you should correct this error.
Between halves of the Harvard-Brown game last Saturday after your interview with Baaron Pittinger, you said:
"I want to thank you, Baaron, for all the assistance you have given to Jim and I."
It is "JIM AND ME." You wouldn't say: I want to thank you for all the help you have given to I. Of course you wouldn't. So you should correct this mistake which you have continually been doing ever since you started play-by-play in Boston.
Practice at home with your wife. Keep saying that over and over again correctly. I want to thank you for helping Ned, Mel and ME. Okay, Ken?
Also, you say during football, "They UNPEEL." What the hell is UNPEEL? Don't you mean: "UNPILE????"

                              Sincerely,
                              J. L.
                              Boston, Massachusetts

And even when Harvard is not involved you have to be careful:

Dear Ken:

Greetings. I am still with you all the way. A common expression in your circle is "a much underrated player." Do we ever hear of a "much overrated player"?

Next time you are tempted to say "therapy treatments" you could save yourself a little by omitting "treatments," because therapy means treatments. And that's the truth.

And don't say congradulations.

> *Yours,*
> *R. I. G.*
> *Pelham, Massachusetts*

I don't often solicit mail over the air, but one night we had a game with the Angels in Anaheim that went into extra innings and ended at 3:55 A.M., Boston time. As we were signing off I said I'd appreciate hearing from anyone who has stayed up so late and would care to write and tell us about it. It's a good thing I added that I would not be able to answer all the letters. There were hundreds, including the ones that follow:

Dear friends:

My usual station—WKNE of Keene, N.H.—does not carry the late games so I had to fish around to find that game that ended at 3:15 A.M. last night. Finally got it on WNHS-FM of Manchester, N.H.

I'm glad I don't have to rise early in the morning because here I am again tonight and I'll be here tomorrow night too. I have scored all the games so far. I'm a seventy-three-year old widow and the broadcasts are about my only recreation now that I cannot attend the games. Thanks so very much for everything.

> *Sincerely,*
> *Mrs. E. H. H.*
> *Springfield, Vermont*

Dear Mr. Coleman:

I listened to the Red Sox game Monday night until 3:15
A.M. Tuesday morning. After the 14th inning I got so ex-
cited I couldn't go to sleep until it ended. I was so mad
the Red Sox lost I went fishing. I am now listening to the
Tuesday night game and Bill Lee has just lost his contact
lenses. I love the Red Sox. I'm twenty-three years old.

> *B. G.*
> *Norwich, Connecticut*

P.S. Scotty just singled in two runs.

Dear Ken:

I was horrified to learn that the game Monday night
didn't end until 3:30 A.M. I knew it was late but all the
lights were out and I couldn't see the clock. I'm not sure
whether or not I qualify for sticking through to the bitter
end. I shut off the radio several times, knowing how soon
8 o'clock comes around, but just couldn't stand the sus-
pense and switched it on again.

I don't know what good it did me though. By the time
it was over, my brain was so fuzzy, and Tuesday morning
I couldn't remember who won the game. Not that it really
matters—our Red Sox win or lose—we love 'em.

> *Sincerely,*
> *B. M. P.*
> *Fairhaven, Massachusetts*

Well, I guess you get the idea. The fans in New England
love the Red Sox, and they also let me know what kind
of a job I'm doing.

Whatever form the letter takes, at least you know that
somebody out there is listening, and that you're making
contact.

CHAPTER 15

Playback

The players and the plays, the teams and their coaches, have spun past my broadcasting booth through the years. It is somewhat disconcerting to see a gray-haired man come to the plate in an old-timers' game and realize I was once describing his exploits—only the day before yesterday it seems.

Games that seemed so important when they were being contested have blended into a kaleidoscope of memories, and the list of athletes I've watched is approaching the size of a telephone directory.

Still, some games, some players, some memories stand out. Here are a few:

I had first seen the kid in a batter's box some years earlier, a willowy left-handed hitter from San Diego, digging in and squeezing the bat until you thought it might turn to sawdust. I was then a high school student, sitting in the Fenway Park bleachers.

Now, twenty years later on a rainy, misty night at Cleveland's Municipal Stadium, I was on the microphone describing Ted Williams' five hundredth major league home run.

It was a hot muggy day in Kansas City and Early Wynn

was pitching. He was old and fat and nowhere near the pitcher he once was, but the competitive juices were still flowing. Several times Wynn had tried and failed in an effort to win his three hundredth major league game, but he wouldn't quit till he had it.

Wynn pitched only five innings that day—five sweat-filled, struggling innings, but they were enough. He left with a one-run lead after five. Jerry Walker relieved, and held the lead over four tense, dramatic innings, as I told the people back in Ohio that this was a historic baseball day—the day Early Wynn won his three hundredth, and final, game.

Herb Score, the best left-hander in baseball, the man said to be worth a million dollars in a trade—leaned in for the sign.

Score was pitching against Gil MacDougald, the fine infielder on the great Yankees teams of the middle fifties. He fired a blazing fast ball, MacDougald hit a savage line drive, and Score was never the same pitcher again.

The drive smacked the left-hander in the left eye and bounded toward the third baseman, who threw Mac-Dougald out. You could hear the crack of the ball against Score's face all the way up in the radio booth.

The pitcher toppled to the ground, blood pouring from his nose and ears. His life was spared, and he tried pitching again in later years, but was never the man with the great fast ball and so much promise.

The city was Baltimore, on a June night in 1959, and Cleveland outfielder Rocky Colavito was furious. A fan had spilled beer on him as he went to his position in right field. Two hours and four pitchers later I had described his fourth home run of the game. Only two others in the his-

Herb Score and I try our hand at squash. *Photo by UPI*

tory of the American League—Lou Gehrig and Pat Seerey
—had ever hit four homers in one game.

And then the city was Boston, and it was the Impossible
Dream of 1967, the year Carl Yastrzemski had the best
single season I ever saw on a baseball field.

In the last two games that season, games the Red Sox
had to win, Yastrzemski had seven hits in eight at-bats. I
was standing in the locker room watching the TV monitor
as Rich Rollins of the Twins popped to Rico Petrocelli
to assure the Red Sox of at least a tie for the pennant.

The players came pouring into the room, shirts torn by
the fans, who had mobbed them on the field. Some of the
players were crying and some were yelling, and I was trying to interview them amid the clamor. Then, when that
excitement subsided, there was the tenseness of listening
to Ernie Harwell report the Angels' victory over the Tigers
—a win that gave the Red Sox the championship and
champagne.

Earlier in 1967, I watched a kid pitcher named Billy
Rohr, in his first major league start, almost achieve baseball immortality. He had a no-hitter going into the ninth
and Yastrzemski preserved it with a spectacular catch of
Tom Tresh's drive into the canyon that is left-center field
in Yankee Stadium. Then, with two out, Elston Howard,
the same Elston Howard who would join the Red Sox later
that season, broke up the no-hitter with a sharp single to
right.

There were more than eighty-six thousand fans on a
September afternoon in 1954 when I broadcast a doubleheader in Cleveland's Municipal Stadium. This was then
the largest crowd ever at a baseball game. Bob Lemon and
Wynn beat the Yankees in the doubleheader, and to all

intents and purposes, the pennant race was over that
people-packed Sunday. Yet, the Tribe went on to win 111
games, a record that still stands.

And there are football memories . . . describing Otto
Graham as he led his Cleveland Browns into a championship game every year of the ten he spent as a pro . . .
watching Lou Groza kick three first-period field goals to
beat the fired-up Steelers . . . seeing a kid quarterback from
the University of Louisville in his first pro game. The
quarterback's name was John Unitas.

And there was Jimmy Brown. People remember Jim
for his many spectacular long runs, and so do I. But I saw
him play every game as a pro, and what I remember most
is how in the closing stages of a game—when the Browns
needed the tough short yardage and everyone knew he
would be carrying the ball on just about every play—he
would get the job done. He was amazing to watch as he
crunched and battered his way, always in control.

It was November of 1968, with a minute to play and
Yale leading Harvard, 29 to 13, and many in the crowd
were leaving the stadium.

But Harvard came back to score twice and I roared into
the microphone as Vic Gatto caught the conversion pass
that gave the Crimson a 29 to 29 tie in a contest voted one
of the five best college football games of all time.

I remember Columbus, Ohio, on a crisp fall afternoon
amid the pageantry of Buckeye football . . . Paul Brown
pacing along the sidelines in a Browns game . . . Marion
Motley smashing for yardage . . . Hugh McElhenny running in a broken field . . . Joe Schmidt backing up a line.

I remember high school teammate Dick Donovan win-

ning his twentieth game for the Indians in 1962 . . . Harry
Agganis playing quarterback for Boston University . . .
Paul Warfield catching a pass in a crowd . . . Mickey
Mantle getting a standing ovation in his last game at
Fenway Park . . . Jim Hegan surrounding a foul ball . . .
the artistry of Whitey Ford on a pitchers' mound . . .

I remember Sunday afternoon and the wind whipping off
Lake Erie as the Giants and Browns battled before eighty-
four thousand at Cleveland's Municipal Stadium . . . Bobby
Layne driving the Lions down the field . . . Horace Gillom's
punting . . .

As the years roll past, you see the athletes from a different perspective. When you begin broadcasting, the men
are your age. You go for a drink with Bob Lemon, Mike
Garcia, and Early Wynn. You attend team parties with
the Browns on Sunday nights and rehash the game with
the guys who played it. You are almost one of them.

But the seasons march along and the players are now
younger than you, so you don't fraternize as much. Lopez
and Stengel and Dykes and Dressen were the managers, but
now they're dead or retired, and men younger than you are
running ball clubs. Even the umpires are younger—and
where did it all go?

You kid Johnny Pesky and Mel Parnell about watching
them play for the Red Sox when you sat in center field as
a high school boy. You're just making jokes, but the fact
is, it is true—these men were once your heroes and now
they're your colleagues.

The train rides out of Arizona—stopping in Wichita
Falls and Paris, Shreveport and Columbus, Georgia—
those days are dim—but you remember that the Indians
and Giants, the New York Giants, please, went along on
the same train. The Giants were run by Durocher and
there was a kid on the club named Willie Mays.

The seasons come and go and you remember the high spots. Pushed into a corner are the lonely days and nights in hotel rooms, and the long walks out of dreary, empty stadiums after the lights had been turned off and the fans had gone home.

When you think about the whole package you feel pretty good inside. There has been so much and much more lies ahead.

A tough, competitive business? Tension and pressure every day? Sure, but I'll take more of the same, thank you, because I never had it so good.

CHAPTER 16

How Do You Get Started?

I've tried to answer some of the questions a potential sportscaster might have. Which brings us to the most important question of all: How do *you* get started?

First, you are going to be told, even as I have warned people, that sportscasting is a small, highly competitive field in which there are few job opportunities.

More and more, former athletes are stepping off the playing fields and into the booth, because they already have well-known, marketable names. This makes it extremely tough on the recruit trying to break in and on the man in the small station who is trying to advance.

You will look for a job and run into the two-edged sword familiar to a young job aspirant no matter what field he's trying to crack. You will be told that a station is looking for a man with experience, but you can't get experience without a job. It's industry's version of *Catch-22*.

I mention these factors so you'll have no illusions in trying to nail down that first job. I do this because it's important to develop an attitude that will help you hang tough.

I once took an audition at a radio station in Gardner, Massachusetts. After I finished, the program director told me I had no chance to make it in the broadcasting business. I should, he suggested, look elsewhere for a living. I chose not to believe him.

Take all the auditions you can, because each time you should get better at it. But don't be discouraged if you don't get a job right away.

Once of the most difficult facets of being a broadcaster is that your product is yourself. You're not selling cat food, or nuts and bolts, or any manufactured product with a set function and price.

When your product is rejected, it is a rejection of you, no matter how diplomatically it's handled, and this is not easy to take. It is necessary to be a realist. If you get enough honest, frank, professional opinions stating that you don't qualify for the job, you must reach a point where you make a decision. Reject the opinions of family, relatives, and close friends. They don't want to hurt you, so their opinions, in addition to coming from amateurs, will be neither honest nor frank.

Every aspiring sportscaster I have ever known, however, has strong feelings about the business. Broadcasting sports is something he dearly wants to do, and money is not the motivation. It is important that, in spite of the obstacles I have pointed out, you give the job search your best shot, so that when the smoke has cleared you'll be at peace with yourself. Too many who have a strong desire to follow a certain path compromise and rationalize and never give themselves a fighting chance.

There is no magic formula to getting the job. The best way to start is to simply knock on doors. Too often the applicant feels the doors will not open. But they will, not always, but most of the time. Radio and television stations, remember, are in the communications field. They will communicate with you, give you time and a fair shake.

I've had experience as a program director on the small-market level and can tell you that most small stations are interested in auditions and tapes because there is a constant turnover. If a man working on a small-market station is good, he will be looking elsewhere once he has established himself. He will be moving toward the bigger ponds.

There is always the exception. At some small stations— and you should bear this in mind when you begin at one —the working conditions are pleasant, the pressures are not great, and there is job security, plus a sense of contributing to the community that is sometimes not found on the major-market level. Some veteran announcers who work in small stations are good enough to be on a higher level, but they are happy with their situation. The money may not be as much but there are other meaningful rewards.

When looking for that first job, write letters to small stations in your area. It is unrealistic to expect to be hired by a big-city station.

Read the help-wanted ads in *Broadcasting* magazine. Submit a position-wanted ad, because executives in the business also read the magazine.

Prepare an audition on tape that will include all phases of broadcasting—news, commercials, ad-libbing, sports, disc jockey work. You will be asked to do all kinds of things in your first couple of jobs.

The fact that you want to be a sportscaster can be a distinct advantage in applying for a job at a small station. The versatility you can offer by being able to do sports as well as staff work is a plus. Many broadcasters are not interested or capable when it comes to covering sports.

If there is a local station in your community, drop in and meet the man in charge. There might be a chance to work part time or as a fill-in for announcers on vacation.

If you're a college student, try to get a job as a spotter or statistician for broadcasters in your area. This is good experience for the day when you'll be doing your own play-by-play. Of course, the college radio station is a natural training ground.

Even if the first job you are offered doesn't call for any sports work, take it. It's much easier to get another job in the business when you already have one; moreover, once you're working you may be able to persuade the boss to put sports shows on the air. In some small stations, you'll be asked to sell, in addition to other duties. I guarantee you that if you sell a sports show, it will get on the air.

Don't be superaggressive or pushy in attempting to land a job. Applying too much pressure is just as bad as applying too little—probably worse.

When you look for a job, be concerned with your personal appearance and grooming. This may be a square attitude in an era of "do your own thing," but the fact is, appearance counts with the men who do the hiring. You are dealing with the public, and other factors being equal, good grooming could be a determining factor in whether you get the job.

Get letters of recommendation from responsible people in your community. It isn't fair to ask a broadcaster whom you may know personally for recommendations based on your ability on the air if that broadcaster has never heard you. Occasionally, students in broadcasting school have asked me questions and I've tried to help them. Then they ask for a recommendation and are surprised when I decline. Certainly I'll give them one based on their character, desire to learn and other attributes. But if I've never heard them on the air or on a tape recorder I am in no position to comment on their work. It is not fair to the prospective employer or to me.

Don't, incidentally, write letters to sports announcers asking, "How do I get in the business?" There is no way these men can write anything more than a perfunctory answer, no matter how accommodating they might want to be.

If you are in high school or college, take any subjects that will help in broadcasting. These would include courses in typing, journalism, English, drama, and speech. Get into the Drama Club, excellent experience for one who wants to spend the rest of his working life before an audience, seen or unseen. A sports announcer, in addition to being a reporter, is a performer, at least in the sense that he is a public figure. You had better get used to that idea.

When you are interviewed for a job at a small station, and the program director asks what sports you can do, reply: "I can do them all." If you are any good, you *can* do them all, by applying what you have learned in this book and by coming up with ideas of your own. Most announcers lean toward one sport, but often you will be called upon to cover many.

After you've worked at a smaller station for a while, you're likely to aspire to a bigger and better job. Have "air checks" made of your work—that is, have a tape recording made of something you've actually done on the air. Preferably this would be play-by-play or your nightly sports show. Even if you work at a college station this can be done.

If you have a friend in the business, don't hesitate to ask him for advice and counsel. He may have contacts that will be helpful. This may open the door for you, but you will still have to get the job and hold it on the basis of your talent.

Along this line, I had a rather embarrassing experience while serving as program director at WJDA in Quincy, Massachusetts. My job was to audition prospective announcers, weeding out the men who had potential so the boss could make the final selection. One day a fellow came through with an excellent audition. He had a deep, resonant voice and read news well. Mostly because of my enthusiasm over the audition, the man was hired.

He went on the air the next Monday but the voice was not the same. "That's not the voice I bought," said the boss, and indeed it wasn't. The fellow had auditioned with a heavy cold, which made his voice mellow and deep. Monday morning the cold was gone, so were the bell-like tones, and shortly afterward, so was he. If you need chronic pneumonia to be a broadcasting success, you're in trouble.

Small stations provide you with a wonderful working education. You'll cover all kinds of events, not specializing in sports, but calling for the same basics you will need in preparing and doing sports full time later on.

At WJDA, under Jim Asher and Joe Tobin, I did a kiddies' program, disc jockey shows, newscasts, ship launchings, panel discussions, quiz programs, telephone-interview shows, remote broadcast interviews at the Weymouth and Marshfield Fairs, and a lot more. In addition there was football, basketball, occasionally high school or American Legion baseball, a daily sports program, and a sports quiz show. The experience was invaluable, and though the work was hard, it was also fun.

Many broadcasters, like writers and actors, are not the same on the air as they are in private life. A person may project over the air as a strong personality, but in private life may be a shy and retiring person whose idea of a swinging evening is a good book and Lawrence Welk. He may live in the spotlight while on the air, particularly in TV work, yet may be the quietest person at the neighborhood cocktail party.

The point of all this is that you should be yourself in a business that has more than the average amount of stress.

When you are on the air you will be wearing your vocal evening clothes and will be doing your job with all the effort and concentration at your command. Much of this will come from your education, your upbringing, and your inner strength and convictions.

Things will happen, of course, over which you have little or no control. Sometimes sponsor conflicts will occur. Suppose you are broadcasting games under the sponsorship of a beer company, and a new beer company takes over. The new sponsor may feel that your identification with the previous company has been so strong that they must make a change. There isn't very much you can do about it—except maybe have a beer and look around for other work.

You will eventually reach the point, without its being any big deal, when you accept yourself as a professional broadcaster. Setbacks will occur, but if you are a pro, you won't allow yourself the luxury of feeling sorry for yourself. This is not unlike the situation with the professional athlete who strives to make it to the majors. There is a period of adjustment before he accepts himself as a major leaguer, no matter how good he may be at playing the game.

Sports announcing is a business of intangibles. Everyone is a listener. That includes the pros in the business, who may listen for different reasons than Joe Fan. The program director may listen for your air presence and sound. The salesman may be listening to hear how you deliver his commercials. The fan is listening because he wants to know what's happening.

Summing it up, the way it will all begin for you will probably make a good story that you'll be able to tell some young announcer thirty years from now. It will be a bit different from anyone else's story, a story that will stand on its own. And that's what makes a sportscaster's job such an interesting way to make a living. You hear it all the time: "Those guys get good money, the best seat in the house. They see the games free, what a deal."

I can't argue with that. It may not be all that meets the eye of the beholder, but it comes pretty close.

Index

ABC sports programs, 124, 125, 128, 132–133
Advertising clients, 106–108
Agganis, Harry, 148
"Air checks," 154
Akron Goodyears, 49
Albert, Al, 127
Albert, Marv, 127
Albert, Steve, 127
Ali Muhammad, 132
Allen, Maury, 74
Allen, Mel, 5, 6, 8–9, 11, 27, 124, 132
American Basketball Association, 127
American Football League, 124
American Hockey League, 96, 127
American League, 98, 99
American League Red Book, The, 20
Aparicio, Luis, 24, 85
Arlin, Harold, 5–6
Ashburn, Richie, 130
Asher, Jim, 155
Associated Press teletypes, 80
Atlanta Crackers, 129
Auditions, 150–152, 154–155
    on tapes, 151–152

Baer, Max, 10
Bailey, Dick, 75–76
Baltimore Colts, 12, 129
Baltimore Orioles, 113, 129
Barber, Red, 6, 9, 10, 24, 27, 129
Barry, Rick, 55
Baseball, 14–31
    consistency and self-discipline, 31
    first telecasts, 10
    information about players, 15–21
    lineups, 21
    play-by-play technique, 15, 22–25, 30
    preparing for, 15–16
    radio coverage, 22–25
    reacting to criticism, 28–29
    scoring and scorecards, 21–22, 28
    small local games, 26–27
    statistics, 22
    styles or techniques, 27–30
    television coverage, 22–25
Baseball Register, 20
Basilio, Carmen, 73
Basketball, 49–56, 113
    color man, 53
    first telecasts, 11

161

Basketball (*Cont.*)
 guests for half-time, 53
 high school championships, 49,
  52–53
 preparing for game, 49, 52–53
  information on players, 52–
   53
  knowledge of rules, 49, 52
  understanding strategy, 49,
   52
 pro games, 55
 radio coverage, 53–56
  giving the score, 54
 spotting boards, 52
 statistics, 53, 55
 television coverage, 54–56
Batting Averages at a Glance, 20
Baylor, Elgin, 114
Bennington Generals, 3–5
"Billboards," cutting, 32
Black announcers, 133
Blass, Steve, 84
Blattner, Bud, 113
Blue, Vida, 97–98
Borza, John, 77
Bosox Club, 109
Boston Braves, 104
Boston Bruins, 57, 86
Boston Celtics, 53–54
Boston *Globe*, 77
Boston *Herald Traveler*, 109
Boston Red Sox, 62, 78, 84, 93
 broadcasting crew, 22–25
 Jimmy Fund drives, 104, 135
 1967 pennant race, 146
 pregame interviews, 101–102
 press book, 16–19
 telecasts, 118
Bowling, 75
Boxing, 72–74, 125–126
 prize fights, 6, 10

Breslin, Jimmy, 11
Brickhouse, Jack, 28, 127
Britt, Jim, 8
Broadcasting magazine, 152
Brooklyn Dodgers, 129
Brookshier, Tom, 43, 114
Brown, Jim, 41, 43, 91, 93, 147
Brown, Paul, 41, 43–44, 147

Camera work, 120
 instant replay, 12–13
 isolated camera, 12–13
Canadian Football League, 128
Capossela, Fred, 74
Caray, Harry, 7, 9, 27, 133
Carpentier, Georges, 6
Cashman, Wayne, 58
CBS sports programs, 121, 126,
  127, 128, 130
Chamberlain, Wilt, 55
Cheevers, Gerry, 57–58
Chicago Cubs, 28, 127
Chicago White Sox, 127
Children's Cancer Research
  Foundation, 104
 See also Jimmy Fund
Christman, Paul, 113, 124
Cincinnati Reds, 130
Clarke, Horace, 24
Cleveland Barons, 96–97
Cleveland Browns, 12, 32–34,
  43–44, 47–48, 77, 147
 sports shows, 90–91
Cleveland Indians, 8, 21, 110,
  117
Cleveland Open, 69
Cleveland *Plain Dealer*, 117, 132
Cloutier, Leo, 105
Coaches, interviewing, 20, 34,
  100
Colavito, Rocky, 29, 114, 144

Coleman, Ellen, 109–110
Coleman, Jerry, 115
Coleman family, 110
Collier, Blanton, 44
Collins, Bud, 77
Collins, Gary, 12
Color men or analysts, 34, 113, 115
  basketball, 53
  football, 41, 43
Commercials, 11–12, 108, 120
  planning use of, 120
Complete Handbook of Baseball, The, 20
Connelly, John, 78
Controversial issues, 81, 84, 87, 99
Cosell, Howard, 132
Cousy, Bob, 98–99
Coyle, Harry, 121
Cramer, Doc, 7
Criticism of officials, 61–62
Culp, Ray, 119
Curry College, 3
Cusick, Fred, 57

Dailey, Bob, 121
Davis, Willie, 114
Delivery techniques
  baseball, 27–28
  basketball, 53, 55
  boxing, 73–74
  golf, 69–70
  rooting for home team, 27–28
Dempsey, Jack, 6
Derogatis, Al, 114
Detroit *Free Press*, 7
Detroit Tigers, 129
DiMaggio, Dom, 109
Directors *see* Producers and directors

Disclaimers, giving, 120
Dodd, Clay, 121
Donovan, Dick, 147
Doral Open, 65
Drees, Jack, 74
Drysdale, Don, 115
Dunphy, Don, 6, 73, 126–127
Durocher, Leo, 148

Elson, Bob, 9, 101, 133
Elston, Gene, 123
Enberg, Dick, 123, 133
Epstein, Mike, 98
Esposito, Phil, 58
Ewbank, Weeb, 44

Fallon, Frank, 8
Falls, Joe, 7
Family life, 109–111
Fans, importance of, 30
Farber, Dr. Sidney, 104
Field, Bryan, 74
Films and film-making, 77–78
  promotion films, 77
  reviewing football plays, 39
  for weekly sports show, 90
Fluffs, broadcasting, 92
Football, 32–48
  camera work, 12–13
  college games, 15, 43
  color man, 41, 43
  coverage of "special teams," 38
  defensive charts, 36
  first broadcast, 5–6
  first telecast, 10–11
  high school games, 41, 43
  judgment and taste, 47–48
  numerical roster, 35, 38
  offensive charts, 36

Football (*Cont.*)
  preparation for broadcast, 34–39
    information on players, 38
    knowledge of rules, 38–39
    reviewing films, 39
  press book, 38
  pro games, 32–33, 43–44
    commercials, 11–12
  radio coverage, 44–46
    position of crew, 44–45
  recreated broadcasts, 10
  spotters, 39–41
  spotting boards, 38
  statistics, 38, 41
  television coverage, 46–48
  "three deep," 38
Ford, Whitey, 148
Foxx, Jimmy, 7
Francona, Tito, 110
Frisch, Frankie (Old Fordham Flash), 8

Gallivan, Danny, 131
Game of the Week, The, 115–116
Garagiola, Joe, 131
Garcia, Mike, 148
Gatto, Vic, 147
Gehrig, Lou, 146
Gifford, Frank, 32, 34, 43, 113, 114, 128
Gillom, Horace, 148
Glickman, Marty, 128
Glover, Fred, 96–97
Golf, 65–71
  anchor man, 67, 69
  announcer's role, 67, 69
  coverage by local stations, 70–71
  dry runs, 67

interviewing golfers, 70–71
network crews, 66–69
practicing technique, 71
preparation for telecasts, 65, 68–69
  background information, 65–66
  camera coverage, 66–68
  producer and director, 67–68
  subdued tone of voice, 69–70
Gowdy, Curt, 6, 14–15, 27, 110, 115, 123–124
Graham, Otto, 114, 147
Graney, Jack, 113
Grange, Red, 114
Green Bay Packers, 32, 34, 47–48, 126
Groza, Lou, 97, 110, 147

Hall of Fame, 21, 116
Halpern, Nate, 47
Hamaleskie, Ray, 75
Hamilton, Milo, 123
Harmon, Merle, 130
Harmon, Tom, 131
Harney, Paul, 84
Harper, Tommy, 23
Harvard-Yale game (1968), 78, 147
Harwell, Ernie, 27, 123, 129, 146
Havlicek, John, 53–54
Hawaii Islanders, 130
Hegan, Jim, 93, 148
Heilman, Harry, 113
Heisman Trophy, 131
Hibbard, Henry, 49
High school broadcasts
  football, 41, 43
  hockey, 58–59
  interviewing athletes, 96

Hiram College, 43
Hoak, Don, 115
Hockey, 57–64
  continuous action, 60
  criticism of officials, 61–62
  description of fisticuffs, 62–63
  high school games, 58–59
  opportunities for announcers, 64
  playmaking, 60
  preparation for game, 57–59
    game strategy, 59–60
    knowledge of players, 57–59
    pronouncing French names, 64
  radio coverage, 60–62
  television coverage, 63
    slow-motion replay, 63
Hodge, Ken, 58
Hodges, Russ, 129
Hoey, Fred, 7
Hornung, Paul, 48
Horse racing, 7, 74, 129
  memorizing colors, 74
Houston Astros, 130
Howard, Elston, 146
Howard, Frank, 99
Hoyt, Waite, 113
Hubbell, Carl, 95
Hughes Sports Network, 75, 121, 126
Hundley, Hot Rod, 114
Husing, Ted, 6
Hussey, Tom, 9

Impossible Dream, The (record), 78
Instant replay, 12–13, 34, 66, 120
  slow-motion, 63

Interviews and interviewing, 93–102
  attitude toward, 96
  with bowlers, 75
  controversial issues, 99
  with football coaches, 100
  with golfers, 70–71
  guests for half-time interviews, 53
  high school athletes, 96
  planning interview, 94
  pregame, 99, 101–102
  putting guest at ease, 94, 96
  questions to ask, 98–100
  during rain delays, 100–101
  research for, 94, 100
  on sport shows, 84, 91
  television, 86, 94–95, 97
  with third base coaches, 98
  with umpires and trainers, 101

Jimmy Fund, 104, 135
Job opportunities, 64, 150
  See also Sportscasting
Jones, Harry, 117, 132

Kalas, Harry, 130
Kaline, Al, 99
Kansas City Athletics, 130
Kansas City Royals, 113
KDKA (Pittsburgh), 5–6
Kell, George, 113, 115
Kelley, Leroy, 12
Kelly, Dan, 127–128
Kelly, Hal, 127
Kelly, John B., 129
Kickoff units, 38
Killebrew, Harmon, 97, 115
King, Nellie, 114–115
Kocourek, Dave, 114
Kono, Morrie, 110

Koster, William, 104
Koufax, Sandy, 115–116, 131
Kubek, Tony, 115
Kusserow, Lou, 14

Lagrotteria, Carlo, 78
Lahr, Warren, 114
Layne, Bobby, 148
Lemon, Bob, 146, 148
Leo, Bobby, 97
Lepcio, Ted, 109
Leroux, Buddy, 101
Letters from listeners, 135–142
    constructive criticism in, 135–
    136
Liberty Broadcasting System, 125,
    133
Linnett, Charles, 36, 51
Little Red Book of Baseball, The,
    20
Lolli, Tony, 121
Lombardi, Vince, 34, 48
Los Angeles Angels, 133
Los Angeles Dodgers, 9

Macauley, Easy Ed, 98–99
McCarthy, Clem, 6, 7
MacDougald, Gil, 144
McElhenny, Hugh, 147
McKay, Jim, 125
McLain, Denny, 99
McNair, Eric, 7
McNamee, Graham, 6
Maguire, Paul, 115
Mainella, Guy, 87, 90
Major League Game of the
    Week, 131
Manchester *Union-Leader*, 105
Mantle, Mickey, 93–94, 148
Marciano, Rocky, 10, 73

Marin, Jack, 55
Martin, Ned, 7, 22–25, 101, 113
Mays, Willie, 148
Mazeroski, Bill, 84
Miami Dolphins, 44
Michaels, Al, 130
Middlecoff, Dr. Cary, 92
Midwest Industrial League, 49
Milwaukee Braves, 130
Minnesota Twins, 130
Mistakes, handling, 40, 92
Mitchell, Bobby, 41
Modell, Art, 90–91
Montreal Canadiens, 131
Moore, Monte, 132
Morris, Johnny, 114
Moses, Jerry, 101
Most, Johnny, 53–54
Motley, Marion, 147
Munday, Bill, 6
Murcer, Bobby, 22, 24
Murphy, Leo, 110
Murray, Jim, 112

NBC sports programs, 14, 73,
    121
NCAA swimming and diving
    championships, 76
NFL championship games, 12,
    15, 77
    1963 Bears and Giants, 47
    1964 Browns and Colts, 12,
    100
    1966 Packers and Browns, 32,
    34
National League, 105
National League Green Book, 20
Neal, Bob, 123
Nelson, Byron, 67
Nelson, Lindsey, 6, 125

New Orleans Open, 65
New York Giants, 124, 128, 129
New York Jets, 130
New York Knicks, 127, 128
New York Mets, 125
New York Nets, 127
New York Rangers, 127
New York Yankees, 62, 84, 93, 124, 131, 132
Nicklaus, Jack, 65, 69–70
Ninowski, Jim, 110
Northern League, 3
Nova, Lou, 10
Numerical roster, 35, 38
Nuxhaul, Joe, 114

Oakland Athletics, 131–132
O'Donnell, Bill, 113
Ohio high school basketball championships, 49, 52
Old–timers' games, 143
Olympic Games, 124, 125
O'Malley, Walter, 9
O'Rourke, Joe, 76, 121
Osmanski, Bill, 47

Pacific Coast League, 130
Palmer, Arnold, 64
Palmer, Bud, 131
Parnell, Mel, 101, 113–114, 148
Paul, Don, 114
Pebble Beach National Open, 66
Perini, Lou, 104
Pesky, Johnny, 22–25, 101, 113–115, 148
Peterson, Fritz, 21
Petrocelli, Rico, 98–99, 137, 146
Philadelphia Phillies, 130
Philander Smith College, 48
Pitts, Elijah, 48

Pittsburgh Pirates, 28, 84, 130
Play-by-play technique, 15
   radio coverage, 22–25
   television coverage, 25–26
Players, background information, 25–26, 52–53, 100
   sources of, 16–21
Porter, Daryl, 119
Pregame activities, 99, 101–102, 118
Press books, 16–20, 38, 100
Price, Jim, 113
Prince, Bob, 7, 8, 9, 28, 130, 132
Producers and directors, 117–122
   approach to game, 121–122
   associate directors, 120–122
   meetings with announcers, 119–120
   responsibilities, 118–119
   role of directors, 117–122
Professional athletes as sportscasters, 112–116, 150

Quarterback Club, The (sports show), 90

Radio broadcasting, 7–8
   baseball, 22–25
   basketball, 53–56
   boxing, 73
   college radio stations, 153
   football, 44–46
   hockey, 60–62
   microphones, 6
   recreated broadcasts, 9
   sports shows, 80–92
Rain delays, 5, 113
   interviews during, 100–101
Rambo, Bob, 76
Ratterman, George, 115

Record-making, 78
Red Sox *see* Boston Red Sox
Reese, Peewee, 14
Referees' decisions, 61–62
Reichardt, Rick, 98
Reifsnyder, Howard, 32
Rice, Grantland, 6
Richert, Pete, 113, 116
Rickey, Branch, 129
Rizzuto, Phil, 8, 113
Robinson, Brooks, 97
Robinson, Frank, 62
Rohr, Billy, 146
Rollins, Rich, 146
Rosewall, Rosy, 8
Rozelle, Pete, 47
Rule books, 20
Russell, Bill, 114
Ruth, Babe, 113
Rutland, Vermont, 3–5, 14
Rutland Royals, 3–5
Ryan, Frank, 100, 110

Saam, Byron, 130
St. Louis Blues Hockey Club, 127
Samel, Joe, 76
Sanderson, Derek, 58
Sauerbrei, Harold, 77
Saxton, Johnny, 73
Schenkel, Chris, 6, 67, 124
Schmidt, Joe, 147
Schneider, Russ, 117
Score, Herb, 95, 113, 132, 144, 145
Scorecards and scoring, 21–22, 115
  baseball, 28
  TV sport shows, 86
Scott, Ray, 6, 32, 34, 125–126
Scully, Vin, 6, 7, 27, 124–125
Seerey, Pat, 146

Shea, Robert, 118–120
Shula, Don, 44
Simmons, Chet, 14
Simon, Jack, 121
Simpson, Jim, 125
Slow-motion replay, 63, 66, 120
Smith, Reggie, 62, 119
Soltau, Gordie, 114
Sound effects, 9–10, 58
Southern Baseball Association, 129
Speaking engagements, 103–106
  presentation, 104
  prespeech pressure, 105–106
Split-screen, 66
Sponsors, 106–108
  conflicts, 156
  "cut the billboards," 32
Sport magazine, 100
Sporting News, 100
Sports Challenge, The (TV show), 133
Sports Illustrated, 100
Sports Network, 65
Sports shows, 80–92
  format for daily show, 82–83
  format for weekly show, 88–89
  fundamental rules, 91
  interviews, 90, 99, 118
  opinions and comments, 85
  play-by-play script, 90
  professional writers, 85
  sponsors, 106–108
  rehearsing, 91–92
  talk shows, 86–89
Sports writing, 109
Sportscasting, 5–6, 150–157
  appearance and grooming, 153
  attitude toward, 150
  auditions, 150–151
  consistency, 31

duties of, 103–111
by ex-ballplayers, 112–116, 150
family life, 109–111
getting started, 150–157
  applying for job, 152–153
  interviews, 154
  letters of recommendation, 153
historical development, 3–13
job opportunities, 64, 150
knowledge of game, 6
listening to other announcers, 91
motivation for, 151
practice techniques, 56, 63, 71, 108–109
qualifications, 6–7, 154
small stations, 78
speaking engagements, 103–104
tension and pressures, 115, 149
variety of assignments, 72, 78–79
verbal trademarks, 8–9
Spotters, 39–41, 152
Spotting boards, 38, 39
Spring training games, 29
Springfield Kings, 127
Station breaks, 120
Statistics, 134
  basketball, 53
  football, 41, 43
  sheets of, 22, 38
Stengel, Casey, 84, 95, 148
Stern, Bill, 6, 10, 126
Stottlemyre, Mel, 23–24
Stuart, Dick, 133
Sugarman, Marvin, 75, 76
Summerall, Pat, 43, 114
Sunset League, 133

Super Bowl telecasts, 126
Swimming and diving, 75–76

Table tennis, 113
Talk shows, 86–89
  role of host, 87
Tape recorders, 27
  for practicing technique, 56, 108–109, 154
Taub, Sam, 10
Television coverage, 7, 11–12
  baseball, 22–25
  basketball, 54–55, 56
  boxing, 73
  compulsory time-outs, 11–12
  first telecasts, 10–11
  football, 46–48
    closed-circuit telecasts, 47
  golf, 65–71
  hockey, 63
  instant replay, 12–13, 34, 66, 120
  isolated camera, 12–13
  make-up, 75
  personal appearance and grooming, 75, 86
  play-by-play, 25–26
  public-address announcing, 47
  simulcasts, 63
  sports shows, 85–86
  use of films and videotapes, 85–86
Tennis telecasting, 76–77
Theatre Network Television, 47
Thomas, Lowell, 80
Thompson, Chuck, 113, 129–130
"Three deep," 38
Time-outs, compulsory, 11–12
Tobin, Joe, 155
Tresh, Tom, 146
Twyman, Jack, 114

Umpiring assignments, 23
Unitas, John, 147
United Press International teletypes, 80
University of Pennsylvania, 76

Verna, Tony, 121
Venturi, Ken, 131
Veterans Job Center of the Air, 3
Videotape recorders, 13, 85–86
Voice, importance of, 6–9
    boxing, 73–74
    golf, 69–70

Walker, Al, 22
Walker, Jerry, 144
Warfield, Paul, 148
Washington Senators, 129–130
WEEI (Boston), 3
Wellman, John, 39
Wells, Don, 123, 133

Western Open, 65
Western Union ticker, 9
White, Bill, 114, 133–134
White, J. Andrew, 6
White, Roy, 24
Who's Who in Baseball, 20
Wilhelm, Hoyt, 97
Williams, Ted, 97, 104, 143
WJDA (Quincy, Mass.), 105, 154–155
WJZ (Boston), 5
WNEB (Worcester, Mass.), 98
Woods, Jim, 131–132
World Series, 6, 14–15, 84
WSYB (Rutland, Vt.), 3
Wynne, Early, 21, 143–144, 146, 148

Yastrzemski, Carl, 4, 24–25, 97, 99, 146
Yawkey, Tom, 104